Verena Gurtner
Gornergrat return

Preface

This is a holiday book. The title is wafted by pure Swiss air and you would be well advised to tuck all thoughts of work and every-day away because we are going to Switzerland; to the mountains of Zermatt to be precise. And this in a most particular way, one with which you may barely any longer be acquainted with: by rail and on top of that with a cog-and-pinion railway!

Holidays and relaxation, that means; occupying yourself with something quite different. For once it could be a cog-and-pinion railway; the one that purrs past the spot where you are drawing a dry stem of grass through your teeth and dreaming into the blue, blue sky.

Yours sincerely V.G.

Verena Gurtner

Gornergrat return

Zermatt - Panorama of a sun-drenched day

100 illustrations
29 in colour
Panoramas and maps
14 tables

Orell Füssli Verlag Zurich

Translated from the German by Paul L. Heller.
Original title "Gornergrat retour - Zermatt, Panorama eines Sonnentages",
Orell Füssli-Verlag Zürich, 1973.
© Copyright 1974 by Dr. Verena Gurtner, 3805 Goldswil-Bern.
Produced by Dr. Verena Gurtner. Printed by Brügger, Meiringen. Lithos
by Aberegg-Steiner, Bern.
Printed in Switzerland
ISBN 3 280 00632 5

Contents

Thirty Fourthousand-metre Peaks and the Box Seat

Truly, a great deal all at once, just think of it, it is similar as with the croaking ravens which one counts to the song-birds. No, the fourthousand metre peaks forming the arena of Zermatt are not so fastidiously catalogued. Admittedly, four of them are perched like jackdaws in the mountain wind on the airy ridge of the Nadelgrat. But with slabs, crags, cracks, chimneys and walls the points cluster to respectful peaks. Here are also Castor and Pollux, the Siamese twins with one body and two heads, and, but this is a special case, the Monte Rosa – all the rest are really mountains according to the book: Cones, lonely and majestic with cone and peak soaring above the clouds.

And yet, not quite, as if each one knew of the other, as if they had secretly conspired, they form a circle instead of the usual chain. They face a common centrepoint, the Gornergrat.

Thus the Gornergrat, similar to a box seat in front of a circular stage within a distance of barely 15 kilometres, is faced by the whole classically considered backdrop of wonderful high mountain ranges, a third of all fourthousand-metre peaks in Europe. In spite of their nearness, none of the great mountains would dream of throwing their shadow on the view-point to overwhelm it. This features the character of this wide ridge: it stands free and un-hampered. Without danger anyone of sound limb can walk around on the Alpine pastures and make contact with the peak of his choice.

Should, however, somebody express the opinion that with greater height and farther view, more peaks would be included in the picture and with them rivers, towns, lakes and foreign valleys, he should be reminded of the difference which gapes between the clear painting of a master and the dis-arrayed heap of a child's coloured building blocks. The effect is achieved by the segment and the proportions of the landscape, in forms and colours, by lines and flourish, in the exactly precise angle and distance to the object. Itself, wide and short-limbed, the Gornergrat is an artist in the field of aesthetics. The dominating southerly stage is kept at bay by the mighty

This is how Zermatt is surrounded by glaciers and 4000-metre high mountains. The valley floor drops down to Visp with a length of 45 km and nearly 1000 metres difference in height.

Double page overleaf: The advanced box-seat of the Gornergrat provides a free panoramic view of the whole mountain chain of Zermatt. The following colour plates on pages 11, 30/31, 18, 14/15, 102/103, 106, 96, 98 repeat the panorama. Detailed information on heights are to be found on pages 56/57 and 101.

Strahlhorn · Stockhorn · Station 3405 m · E · Cima di Jazzi · Weissgrat · Weisstor · Gornergl.

Schwarztor · Roccia Nera · Breithornzwillinge · Breithorn · Chli Matterh. · Testa Grigia · Theodulpass · Theodulh.

Wellenkuppe · Trifthorn · Rothornhütte · Zinalrothorn · Schalihorn · Mettelhorn · Weisshorn 4505 m · Brunegghorn · Blümlisalp · N

Gorner glacier – the mightiest of the Alps after the Great Aletsch glacier – like the farsighted holds his newspaper at arm's length. In the East and North the flat bowl of the Findelen glacier keeps the mountains at a distance, similarly as the Piazza before the chased marble of a cathedral.

Even if glaciers swill around the foot of the Gornergrat it does not get cold feet. A warmer footstool than the Riffelalp on its West side and a softer carpet than the flour-bedecked Matter valley can not be found within the surroundings. The stormy winds rebound on the high cliffs of the southerly forward bowl of the valley of Zermatt. Sub-alpine flora, light summer breeze

In 75 years the rack-and-pinion railway has transported 25 million tourists to the 3135-metre high Gornergrat. To the left of the twin-domed Kulm hotel the station of the Stockhorn cable-way which carries on over the whole length of the ridge 250 metres higher up into the world of the glaciers.

Right: The Monte Rosa presents itself in its best dress to the Gornergrat. The Dufourspitze on the right is, as all schoolchildren should know, the highest point in Switzerland, and since 1863 carries the name of Switzerland's first general who also was the creator of the triangulation and the first common set of maps of the cantons belonging to the Confederation.

10

Gornergrat and Riffelhorn in front of the back-drop of Liskamm, Castor and Pollux, Breithorn. The wide plateau-type slope crossed by two flat depressions on the North slope of the Gornergrat is the Riffelberg. The railway gallery is clearly seen on the Riffelbord; at the bottom, Riffelalp.

and a variety of rare butterflies flutter like fairyland magic under the blue sky of the paradise-like landscape and at the edge of the eternal snows.

It is time to take up the reader's question on the special case of the Monte Rosa. To accept the item on the agenda means to lift the veil of intimate relations of the Gornergrat with its opposite and to seek the reasons which led to its railway.

We spoke of the fourthousand-metre peaks. The Monte Rosa is in this respect a topographical rarity because it puts full ten peaks above the magic figure into the pot and was able to set apart each one. The Breithorn, for instance, has two hangers-on, which never figure in any list – two sparrows on the edge of the field.

How can the indelicate favouring of the one and the setting back of the others be explained? Surely only by the fact that after the Mont Blanc the

The terminal station of the Gornergrat railway provides a majestic view over the Gorner glacier and lies free of any obstruction opposite the Matterhorn. In comparison to pages 120/121, the retraction of the Upper Theodul glacier is noteworthy.

Monte Rosa, which is 173 metres lower, carries the highest point of Europe and in addition, just as the potentate of Chamonix and Courmayeur, sits abreast the frontier in the corner of the country. The Monte Rosa is by no means as affable and pure as it presents itself to the inhabitants of Zermatt. In its back it sports a 2000 metre high insidious rock cliff (the biggest of the Alps!), over which avalanches and rock salvoes continuously thunder vertically into the valley of Macugnaga. The back and cliff edge belong to the

Overleaf: Early risers can enjoy the view of the Matterhorn at its finest from the hotel window on the Gornergrat. In July the first rays of the sun touch the clearly exposed East flank of the Furggen ridge, left and the Hörnli ridge, right. A quarter of an hour later the pink hue vanishes and turns into normal daylight. The photograph on the right shows the Dent Blanche, Grand Cornier and Obergabelhorn in the early morning sunlight from the same position. In the shade is the Pointe de Zinal and Mont Durand (Arbenhorn).

→

Above the pines and larches of the Riffel wood and the valley, the view sweeps over the bowl of the Trift with Wellenkuppe, Trifthorn and Zinal Rothorn. The Riffel wood prides itself with 500 to 1000-year old trees and that at a height considerably higher than the average tree-line in Switzerland. With a height of 2400 metres, the tree-line here is probably somewhat higher than anywhere in Europe.

Italians, the Valaisans, however, could not abstain to compensate their friends with a few border peaks and a share of the better part of the mountain as in any case three–quarters of it is based on southern ground and in the worst case knolls and protrusions on a ridge can be exploited as peaks. It is to be noted, however, that the worthy Swiss, loyally following the example of the clever Savoyards, had previously reserved the highest peak to themselves. The frontier here as there runs 50 metres below the peak on the neighbour's side!

The kindly Piedmontese at the foot of the mountains were cheated of the highest points of their two glacier-bound rock bastions which glitter over the green plain. Yet, for all that, say the fishermen, the reflection of the Monte Rosa shines in the lagoons of Venice on clear days!

This giant is thus the nearest neighbour to the Gornergrat and the old inhabitants of Zermatt from their viewpoint called it simply the "Gornerhorn". Indeed, they were able, with the most famous mountain in the world to bring their village to everybody's door-step but luck was not in favour of the "Gornerhorn". Similarly to the Liskamm, the Monte Rosa obtained its cartographic name in the other valley. Monte Rosa is derived from the

Present Installations of the Gornergrat Railway

Stations and stops (H)	Height above Sea level, m	Distance from Zermatt, km
Zermatt Bahnhof	1604	—
Findelenbach (H)	1770	1,8
Riffelalp	2210	4,0
Riffelboden (H)	2348	5,1
Riffelberg	2582	6,5
Rotenboden (H)	2819	7,9
Gornergrat	3089	9,3

Start of construction mid-May 1896, Inauguration 20.8.1898.

Aosta "roisa", the glacier, and Liskamm from the French vallée de Lys , the valley of the white lilies.

Together with the poetic names came the first alpinistic advances to conquer the border range from the other side. With a following of scientists, mountain guides and porters with cooking pot and tent, sketch-book and barometer they climbed from Gressonay, Alagna and Macugnaga; Vincent, Zumstein, Giordani, Parrot, Gnifetti and Ludwig von Welden. They crossed over saddles and passes of the Monte Rosa as were they thresholds of a castle. And as others leave the impression of their soles on the flagstones, the names of the first climbers imprinted themselves in the nomenclature of the maltreated mountain range. But for the highest peaks the time was not yet ripe. Suitable equipment and advanced accommodation was lacking. (See map page 99).

Until the approach to the border range was sought from the North and, hesitatingly, one became acquainted with a night's resting place in the rocks at the Gorner glacier and accepted the possibility of overcoming the endless ice-falls, decades had gone by. Only in 1847 the first alpinists reported an attempt to climb the Monte Rosa from the Zermatt side. But already in 1855, that is 79 years later than on the Mont Blanc, the first roped team put their feet on the "Highest of them all". A better sounding name was not known for the time being for the peak which was later to be named the

The first morning sun touches the Breithorn. The climb to the main summit is round the back over the Theodul pass and is considered by mountaineers as the easiest climb of a 4000-metre mountain. The North flank, here seen from the Gornergrat, is no child's-play.

Dufourspitze. That trip had begun under the larch door of the Riffelberg guesthouse which had been opened the year before with 18 beds!

"The more a man gets, the more he wants" – the desire to conquer this unknown world of mountains was driven to the peak following the success on the Monte Rosa. From the richly laid table of Alpine feats the caviar and salmon were picked and the vegetables swallowed in order not to lose the habit of eating. After the Dufourspitze; Nordend, Allalin and Mischabel vanished from the dish, Rimpfischhorn, Alphubel, Liskamm and the twins; after the Weisshorn and the Dent Blanche, followed the Dent d'Hérens, Zinal and Obergabelhorn. Within a decade the approachability of all the high peaks within the circle of Zermatt, including the Matterhorn was proven. A few peas spilt over the fork and were swept up years later: Hohberghorn, Lenzspitze, Dürrenhorn and Bishorn.

The pine or cembra-pine is distinguished by its five-needle tufts. With long-extending, snake-like roots it manages to hold itself on to rock and dry steep slopes where other trees can no longer exist.

The more acquainted the local guides became with the surroundings the surer they became in guiding their guests. Handymen of science had become squires of the mountains and the scientists developed into tourists. What did the followers care to climb the ladder of the skies over worn-out steps? The rich adventure – stamping the snow first, danger, fellowship, new paths, ridges, cliffs and above, the wide dome of the firmament changing from night to day and from light to dusk – continued. Mountaineering had become the fashion. Willpower and boundless vigour, protest and the high aims of the young – what price the world – led to deeds. From the stuffiness of bourgeois sitting-rooms, from offices, school forms, shops and fatherly guardianship they fled into the pure air of the mountains. Dividends and hard-won savings changed hands for a pair of nailed boots: – In the Alps the "Rock and Roll era" had taken over.

Mirrors, Mirrors everywhere

Little lakes are strewn on the Gornergrat and over the Riffelberg, they play with mountains as if they were balls. One is not enough. You jump here and catch the Monte Rosa, walk there and the Matterhorn flies towards you, you think to touch the Weisshorn and fall into the Zinal Rothorn. They make fools of those who were of sound mind and enchant those who came to see. Winners are always the little waters. In order to supply humanity flowing from the towns and cities for the sake of the mountains with such earthly necessities as food, drink and wide beds, the newly built Riffelhaus was soon too small. For already here on the threshold the prickling sensation of the venture creeps under the skin: shortly after one o'clock in the morning the companions step out into the night on the big adventure, plod silently, step by step following the lantern of the guide over the grass and scree, wet with dew, uphill. The ring of an ice-pick against a rock breaks the silence, a hushed word is spoken. Pale and serenely the dusk swathes the shadows of the mountains, the mirror of the Riffel lake begins to radiate. Grass stems rock restlessly in the water and, shimmering, a pyramid breaks in pieces in the ruffled glass, it contracts, breaks apart, flows together, diverges, coagulates and vanishes. It was a wisp of fog.

Standing immovable above it all the demon, the rock which emerges out of the belt of glaciers, solitary, on the other side of the valley. Its black cliffs threaten, the ridges indistinct in their form. The mountain waits ghost-like; for whom? You can feel it threateningly in the small of your back, turn around and can barely tear away from the sight to direct your eyes to your aim in the silver-shimmering knolls above on the glacier. In the warmth of the sun, however, you return with heavy limbs, the ghostliness and fear of the night gone. The little lakes delight in their games, the Matterhorn generously beckoningly throws the symmetry of its body over the surface. "Am I not beautiful?"

A vampire, groaned the reporters. One, who wanted to make sure, who itched to put paint to canvas was the young Whymper from London. Edward was 20 years old when he first came to the Riffelberg and put the telescope to his eye. "Cut up wood", he had written in his diary. Wood-carving was quite a current profession since the book and newspaper publishers had discovered that pictures promote the sale of their products. The art consisted

"Mirror, mirror, say, am I the finest mountain?" The Matterhorn self-consciously regards itself in the Riffel lake on the Gornergrat. It has every reason to be satisfied with itself and with the mirror.

Above the valley of Zermatt and over the Gorner glacier lies the throne of the Gornergrat, an unimpressive ridge, which, however, thanks to its central position amidst the high mountains surprises with its unexpected beauty of its panorama. Right in the shade of the cloud, the Riffelhorn in front of the Monte Rosa and Liskamm, left the eternal snow-basin of Findelen.

in transferring the illustration to be duplicated inversely on to the wooden printing blocks and to extract the contours carefully with the graving tool from the sunk base. "Drew diagrams, etc. Diagrams! Oh, sickening job. I have to draw lines frequently one-sixth of an inch thick and that for many weeks together. Oh, how I should rejoice to escape from this thraldom with scarcely any prospect of better times......"

Help, where is help? It was not the order of the day to give vent to one's feelings by organised 'sit-ins', 'sit-downs' and 'squattings' in protest but in contrast, as we have seen, climbing had been discovered. Whymper had found his way to the Alps and was determined to give his urge for opposition a free hand on the cliff face and was resolved to obtain the last morsels of caviar and salmon. In other words to set his foot to the best rock, the un-

Also the Matterhorn can be humble, it depends where one stands. In the reduced perspective from Höhbalm even the North wall and Zmutt ridge lose their frightening appearance. Left, the Hörnli ridge through which the railway constructors had planned a tunnel in 1890. The approach was coupled to that of the Gornergrat.

touched Weisshorn or the Matterhorn. For once he wanted to be the first. His compatriot Tyndall beat him to the white peak – so there remained the Obelisk. During the course of five years Whymper tackled it eight times, always from the Breuil side. The attempts of the coolly calculating climber were, however, not the only ones. Prior to all, the Italian Carrel had become entangled in the net of temptation and there resulted an un-praiseworthy race which culminated in a heated struggle. The cautious Zermatt guides shook their heads and pointed to the wild eastwardly-pointed

Overleaf: On the ascent to the Matterhorn. Behind the Stockhorn and Gornergrat rise the Rimpfischhorn, Strahlhorn and Cima di Jazzi. Bottom left, the Hotel Belvédère in front of whose windows the normal route, the approach to the Hörnli ridge, begins. →

crags of the giant rock. How could that be crossed? This was reason enough for young Whymper to be of a different opinion, particularly as it was his profession to think contrarywise. His decisive expedition followed, prepared in all haste and coincidence, put together among friends and their guides and as on the Monte Rosa, ten years previously, in spite of all from the Zermatt side.

The first ascent of the Matterhorn and the accident which took toll of four young people (a rope broke) resulted in a storm of indignation in all industrial countries. "Martyrs of fashion", "absolute madness", were the mildest of words which were found. The result, however, was serious and unexpected. "One" hurried to Zermatt to see this place of catastrophic temptation with one's own eyes. Even before the first people had set foot on the ridge of the Matterhorn in 1865, the Riffelberg inn had to be enlarged to 30 rooms; now, the Riffelhaus and the Gornergrat became a playground. It was certainly not the fault of the inhabitants of Zermatt if the Matterhorn had become an object of trade: the price is set by supply and demand.

It was a short step from the crowds of pilgrims to the peak and the caravans to the Gornergrat to the project of the railway. The rails were already approaching the Alpine resort from Visp. Under the dome of the Federal

On the terrace of the Kulm hotel Gornergrat the panorama, fresh air and life in the warm sun can be enjoyed. Whoever wishes, walks over the extensive pastures and finds solitude in wonderful spots wherever he likes.

Palace in Bern, however, it required a double take before one had realised what the pamphlet under a purple cover contained which had been submitted to the authorities in August of 1890. It asked for nothing less than the

Main Characteristics of the Gornergrat Railway and Comparison with other Railways

Main characteristics	Gornergrat	Brig-Visp-Zermatt	Furka-Oberalp	Chamonix-Montenvers
Top station, metres a.s.l.	3089	1605	2160, 2033	1909
Max. diff. in height, m	1485	955	2085	879
Operational length, km	9,3	44	96,7	6
Gauge, cm	100	100	100	100
Adhesion, Rack-rail	R	AR	AR	R
Rack-rail type	Abt	Abt	Abt	Strub
Steepest gradient in %	20	12,5	11	22
Power system	3-phase 50 Hz	1-phase alternate 16 2/3 Hz	1-phase alternate 16 2/3 Hz	1-phase alternate 50 Hz, Diesel
Contact line voltage	725	11 000	11 000	11 000
Inauguration	1898	1890-91	1914-26	1909

approval to "a comfortable connection from the Zermatt station which is under construction with two main view-points, Gornergrat and Matterhorn in order to facilitate their approach» (Heer, application for concession of 20. August 1890). Four weeks later a second application of the same contents landed in the form of six sheets on the desk of the Councillors (Roten, Zen Ruffinen and von Ernst, application for concession of 22. September 1890). And this at a time when only the keen inhabitants of Zermatt trusted their lives to the new steam vehicle which moved between Visp and Stalden, whereas all the others prayed to heaven when they set eyes on that thing! Summersaulting and standing on one's head is not a thing for the Swiss. Each thing in its place is his motto. To be of varied opinion on a railway to the Gornergrat was absolutely justified, concerning the Matterhorn, however, this time one stood on one's head. The project was recommended by the Federal Council and approved with decisive majority by Parliament (Imfeld and Heer, concession of 20. June 1892).

The Eiffel tower was haunting the world. As the great attraction of the Paris World Exhibition of 1889, the 300-metre high steel scaffold appeared to fulfill all the promises that were demanded of engineering. In the same year the news made the rounds of the world press that it was intended to tunnel through the Jungfrau near Interlaken and to build a railway to the 4158 m high peak. Should therefore the Matterhorn step aside? Surely not. The

program of the "Zermatt high alpine railways" was not less exciting. The ambitious plan comprised an approach from Zermatt to the foot of the steep inclines and subsequently a Gornergrat line and a Matterhorn line. Each section was split in accordance to incline and terrain into sections with various operational systems. The traveller was expected to submit to an exhausting series of changes. Fortunately, such plans are often short-lived for it would have been wise to leave coat and cane at home rather than to forget them in a carriage.

You are curious how this railway would have looked? Then why don't you bring your family, we'll start right away! Possibly we can remain seated in the carriage as far as Zermatt because the "High alpine railways" are operated with the same traction as the valley railway from Visp as far as the valley bowl passing underneath the village hill – steam and cog-rail with inter-

Left: The first project for the "Zermatt high alpine railways" saw a common approach to the foot of the steep ramps and from there a system of railways to the Gornergrat and to the summit of the Matterhorn. The construction of the last section of the Matterhorn railway was bound to the condition of proof of the safety for workmen and passengers. The concession was never taken up, expired and has not been renewed from an environmental point of view. The Gornergrat railway could, however, after a change of the original plans be built and from the start enjoyed great popularity.

Double page overleaf: The Gornergrat railway leads close past the great glaciers. View from Kulm to the Liskamm, 4527 m, Felikjoch, Castor and Pollux, the 4228 and 4092-metre twins above the morainback of the "Schwärze". Left and right of the Liskamm flow the Grenz and Zwillings glaciers.

→

mediate adhesion sections. At the latest at the station "Gorge" at the entrance to the Gorneren gorge, it must be decided whether we first wish to go to the Matterhorn or to the Gornergrat. While the train continues in the direction of the weatherbeaten brown houses of the hamlet Zum See, the unhooked carriages with the passengers for the Gornergrat return by means of a hairpin turn and small locomotive on the flat along the other slope as far as "Moos". The station forms the starting point of the electric funicular to the Riffelalp and lies at the foot of the West steep ramp close to the wood. Our cabin is drawn up in a straight line through rhododendrons, larches and pines. But before butterfly net, parasol and picnic basket have been stored under the bench, the change-over station with large wheel and steep steps at half cable-length already appears. The funicular with motor in the middle of the distance is in accordance to the new example of the Salvatore funicular

near Lugano: at half way one must change into the car coming from the opposite direction. Freshly sorted and boxed-in we now see the Riffelalp approaching. And look, what do we see here, a little garden house on four wheels? An electric rack-rail locomotive! Why is it only waiting here? Exhausted, we let ourselves be gently pushed by the humming little summer-

Rolling-Stock and Performance of the Gornergrat Railway

Years	Electric engines	Motor-coaches	Double motor-coaches	Pas-sengers carriages	Capacity, Pas-sengers	Train-km, av. p. year	Passengers conveyed, av. p. year
1898-1902	3	—	—	6	330	9 656	28 095
1903-14	4	—	—	8-9	429-489	12 876	37 862
1915-29	4	—	—	9	489	10 378	29 339
1930-46	5	—	—	9-8	489-429	20 983	60 776
1947-51	5	2	—	7	770	41 650	192 840
1952-54	5	4	—	6	880	61 313	300 285
1955-58	5	6	—	6	990	101 645	569 222
1959-60	5	8	—	5	1 100	128 772	882 329
1961-65	4	12	—	3	1 320	139 689	1 145 678
1966-72	3	12	2	—	1 800	144 829	1 599 112

house in the open summer carriages over sunny alpine pastures towards the Gornergrat. The picnic-basket, unfortunately, was left down below!

The complicated itinerary was, and quite rightly, only realised on this side of the valley and that only in its upper part. The Gornergrat railway did not become the first electric rack-and-pinion railway of the world as it could have been (this distinction was claimed by the railway on the Mont Salève), but certainly the first in Switzerland. Before it could be built, however, it had to rid itself of the Matterhorn railway. Down to the foot of the great rock the Matterhorn railway had been similarly planned like the line to the Gorner-grat: following the steam railway there was to be a funicular with an incline of as much as 55% (55 centimetres climb to one metre horizontal length) and then an electric rack-and-pinion railway of 4.5 km. Before we continue our journey you had better take a deep breath. If you have eight children, please take only four along! On a partly open gradient with a 33% incline the railway now climbs along the South slope of the Hörnli along the Furgg glacier. A 200 metre long tunnel goes straight into the flank of the Matterhorn and into the underground station "Whymper's hut" at 3140 metres. Here we change into the funicular which continues on a slope with an average gradient of 75% for the remaining 2300 metres direct to the summit – but no, at half-way one again has to change from one car to another. Here too, the driving motor is in the middle of the distance. The cabins which are supported on steep rack-rails of the Abt type, hang on several cables in the high shaft. They have special devices for a careful speed regulation and multiple braking. In the unlikely case of a break-down or illness the passengers are free to descend the 1345 metres on foot on the stairs which are fitted around the walls of the shaft and have small recesses at short intervals. About 20 metres below the summit ridge of the mountain panorama-galleries, a restaurant and some dormitories are provided so that there is no reason for a hurry to return from the peak.

This was the Matterhorn railway according to the conception of the Federal Parliament of 1892. The nightmare (it turns up periodically) had, however, been restricted to the extent that the constructors were bound by the condition that prior to an approval of the detailed plans proof had to be given that construction and operation of the railway "does not provide any exceptional danger in respect to life and health of persons". By this was meant the great dangers of great height. The technical execution basically gave no reason for worry and whether the Matterhorn railway was suspended on cables or hopped on an air cushion was primarily of no importance. The

When the last train has left the Gornergrat the quiet remaining tourist may come across a small miracle: Calmly the Ibex approach, lightly they walk across the railway square as if it were their living room. There is a herd of some sixty head of these shy animals in the rocks around the Riffelhorn and the South wall of the Gornergrat.

second plan which had been submitted as a variation had, with emphasis, referred to a recently published article in the Swiss construction journal by Locher of Zurich who built the Pilatus railway, in which he had suggested a new procedure for the Jungfrau railway: two parallel tunnels in which the passenger carriages, guided in three rails were simply shot to the peak on a column of compressed air. Locher was prepared to try this also on the Matterhorn. Strangely enough, also in this second project provision was made for a junction of the two railway lines, this time at the station "Moos". However, the originators must have been aware of the sigh of the tried head of the family for they brought the two rack-and-pinion railways, here operated by steam, down to Moos and did without the funiculars. On the other hand, their budget climbed in view of the considerably longer ramps from SF 7 million to SF 10 million.

The question remains why Parliament favoured the first project, how the nightmare of the Matterhorn locked itself in its haunted castle and the Gornergrat railway was given the all-clear. That is a story of its own, with a frog which is transformed and a dark-eyed maiden. In addition one should first know how Zermatt is constituted.

Horse-drawn carriages are available for anyone at Zermatt station. In 1972 the Citizens' Commune decided in a third and probably final vote to reject the expensive project worked out by the Canton for the extension of the public motor-road to Zermatt. The healthy development of the village would only have suffered, for the guest appreciates just this peace from traffic.

Zermatt with Horses

Attention: this chapter is an historical digression! You may jump the next few pages unhindered. But then you will not understand why the motor road to Zermatt stops at Täsch. You also wanted to know about the back history of the project of the "Zermatt high alpine railways". It is unavoidable to return to the year 999.

Let us begin with that closest at hand. Whoever remains longer than 24 hours in Zermatt will, without fail, be confronted with the ascent of the Matterhorn and secondly with the fact of two types of citizens. In Zermatt there is not only the universal by-partition of human society of male and female, left and right but in addition in citizens and burghers. The quality of the latter is given from the combination of name and descent. From a list of somewhat over twenty family names it is possible to distinguish the burghers as descendants of old Zermatt families. In order to designate the citizens, a telephone directory and the Swiss map is required – in the eyes of the old Zermatters a highly indelicate means of identification. The burghers, therefore, have always lived in Zermatt and the citizens are inhabitants whose place of origin is somewhere else. The burghers form the Burghers' Commune with Council and Council president, burghers and citizens, however, form the Municipal Commune with their President and the bodies common in this country. The burghers have their rightful pride; their ancestors fulfilled an historically

remarkable feat. In the secludedness of their valley, uninfluenced by outside ideas, they had, already at an early stage, rid themselves of the long arm of their masters and built up a free, autonomous commune with independent legislation. In the old days the Bishop of Sion was the squire. By sale and subsequent inheritance his worldly right in the valley of Nikolai fell to three noblemen with whom the inhabitants of Zermatt started negotiations in the 16th Century on compensation of claims on house and land, all respective duties and on the individual person. In three blocks and scarce money it could only have been obtained with great circumspect and iron will to saving, the purchasing contracts were concluded (1538, 1562, 1618). They comprised some 190 households which were situated in the settlements of Ried, Spiss, Haueten, Steinmatten and Winkelmatten, in Herbrigg, Moos, Tufteren, Zmutt, Zum See, Blatten and Furi, even in Schweigmatten, in Den Bächen and in Findelen. A fraction lived around the church. Zermatt had more inhabitants than 300 years later and where you, dear reader, today wander through dry barren land on warm sunny days, there grew rye and later potatoes in artificially irrigated fields.

Following the taking into effect of the agreement the free families formed three political communes, gave themselves similar constitutions and an administrator, who without "judicial fuss" was appointed for two years to "see to justice for all and to eliminate trouble to the best of his ability". At the same time the Matters purchased outright dispensation from the cleric in St. Niklaus for the indebted cattle tithes and with their own parson for the grain tithes. The 'honeymoon' lasted until the attack of Napoleon's army on the Valais and the "citizens" in Zermatt. Shortly before, in 1791, the three communes had quickly formed themselves into one and thrown woods, pastures and mountains, over whose exploitation one fought over notoriously, into the general melting pot. The pot, however, bears the inscription: – attention, only for domiciled Burghers! It is, thanks to this label, that today the alpine pastures, also the Gornergrat, is still owned by the burghers. Otherwise they would most likely have been sold off piece-meal.

As different as the inhabitants of Zermatt may be, basically they all strive for the same end and that is to make progress, only that they do this each in his own individual way. For decades it was only possible to drive or ride with short reins in Zermatt, if there was a horse in the stable. For centuries one went on foot and perhaps one barely owned two pairs of boots. That it

Storey proprietorship has always been known in the Valais. In order to spare the meagre agricultural land and pastures, houses were built into the slopes and constructed jointly by various families. The Zermatt house is joined with massive larch timber, the kitchen is of masonry and the roof covered with flag-like quartz plates. Weatherproofing of the wood is provided by the untiring sun.

was not possible to drive at a canter either out into the world or into the valley was due to the accumulations of snow and rock which build up in the high ravines and principally seriously threaten two passages of the road; one in the steep slopes behind Stalden and the other immediately before arriving at Zermatt. In order to deliver the cattle to the pastor in St. Niklaus, the tenth calf had to be born and also the road put in order. It cost as much to satisfy the welfare of the soul with meat and grain as it cost for the road to the valley. The Zermatters had a hard time with their neighbours in order to keep a connection with the outside world open. The Kennedy who in summer 1861 had unsuccessfully attempted the ascent of the Hörnli ridge and tried to find success in winter, already shortly after Stalden came across serious difficulties on his courageous way. The masonry of the mountain track, stuck on to the South slope had been smashed and dispersed by rock falls and the pressure of the ice and lay in disarray in the cavernous ditch of the Vispe; behind Täsch no less than six avalanches with a depth of up to 70 metres had built up in the gate of the valley. Even in the summer the wanderer had to do without a carriage between Stalden and St. Niklaus. The guests who aimed for Zermatt, the Riffelberg and the Matterhorn had the choice to complete their trip from Visp either on foot, on the back of a sturdy horse or to be transported by two stalwart porters, more roughly than

The main street between church and railway station. The tourist enjoys the rare priviledge to stroll unhindered by motor traffic in the streets and the valley.

in comfort, in a sedan chair. Only from St. Niklaus a horse-drawn carriage awaited the traveller and this only after the instigation of the inn owner Alexander Seiler had achieved the construction of a small road out of the alpine track on the upper reaches of the Vispe and made it possible to be used for one-horse carriages. The Communes below Zermatt could not be persuaded to extend the road beyond the gorge of the Kipfen and the valley barrier of Stalden. The mountain track fully satisfied their meagre requirements and the Canton felt over-generous if they granted the application of the ambitious resort a sum of SF 300 for the upkeep of the path.

The situation was ideal to clear the valley like a fire with the aid of foreign initiative. The manner of the means were less important than the fact that money was collected and people were found who were prepared to undertake the risk. Whether a road is built and taxes collected or a railway is built and fares charged comes, in the end, to the same. For Governmental reasons it had been decided to do away with road taxes and to tie the hands of the railway companies in such a manner as to only enable them to reap a harvest where the crop was abundant. Without a considerable measure of willingness for risk nothing, therefore, happened.

In spite of this, within forty years of the inauguration of the first railway line from Zurich to Baden 3000 km of rails had been laid. With 9.8 km of

Zermatt has become a mountain town. In spite of the exhaust-free traffic the helicopter and rescue teams provide rapid assistance.

railway per 10 000 inhabitants the network in 1886 – the time of the con-
cessioning of the Visp-Zermatt railway – had a higher density than even
in England, France, Germany and Belgium. Indeed, the railways had not
just flown off the drawingboard. The technical breeze found an upwind in

The Development of Zermatt to a Resort

Year	Population	Hotel beds	Hotel guests	Length of sojourn av. days	Travellers to Zermatt
1838		3	12		12
1855	370	90	1 600		1 600
1867	430	176	4 400	20	4 400
1880	492	428	9 300		9 300
1890	550	800	15 000		15 000
1938	1 000	2 469	24 651	5,2	69 400 *
1950	1 395	2 200	37 483	4,5	158 800
1960	2 731	2 936	82 502	5,5	429 600
1970	3 101	4 164	119 210	5,4	715 500

* as from 1938, $^1/_2$ rail frequency accepted.

the economic legislative development in the Federal State. With the Constitution of 1848 the 22 cantons had overcome a mile-stone by moving the
customs to the country's border and had created standard regulations of the
post, coinage (297 local types were in circulation!), measures and weights. If
many believed the arm of the woman on the new silver franc had turned
out too long, money could now flow unhindered through mediation of the
banks to collect where profits promised.
However, the public and the cantons kept a wary eye on the dividend-heavy
railways and feeling ran high among the citizens on the question of "private or
Federal railways". In 1852 a supervisory law was decreed which gave the
Federation competence of control and also laid down repurchasing conditions but otherwise opened the field to competition. The formation of private
railway companies – this was also free to the cantons – as well as the promotion of regional interests was open. The denser, however, that the railway

← Only a small part of the precipitous atmospheric currents from the South cross over the Theodul
pass, Weissgrat and the Col de Valpelline in the protected valley of Zermatt. The climate is
dry and warm. In spite of this the preserving glaciers provide sufficient water in the summer.
View from the Rimpfischhorn on to the Findelen glacier and Matterhorn.

net became in the industrialised plains, the more the main lines thwarted themselves (it had already come to bankruptcies), the keener the initiators turned to the mountain railways which practically exclusively served tourism. In order to restrain the growing rush of speculation and the unsatisfactory conditions in public transport the Federation had to retract its generosity. With the passing of the railway law of 1872 it was given the right of granting concessions and the newly formed department was charged with the supervision of construction and operation of the railways, the equipment and finances, the statutes, the time-tables and the fares. To have decided in Bern whether a railway may be built on their territory was not at all to the taste of the Valaisans. Guardianship is about the last straw that they would be burdened with. Who are these Valaisans?

In any case real Swiss, measured from their imagination of the purgatory and they supply the water to the four cantons on the Lake of Lucerne – incidentally this flows to both sides of the Furka from the same mountain. Only, the Valais joined the Confederation 500 years later than Uri, Schwyz and Unterwalden. Time was not sufficient to mutually wear off edges and corners which makes life bearable.

Indeed, the Upper Valais communes had already at an early stage come to agreements with the Central Swiss. The agreements in the end aimed at the defense of the Alps against the mutual neighbours in the South, the mighty Duke of Milan. One did not wish to bind oneself for more than 10 years, as for one, the renewal of the documents on both sides always gave rise for a pleasurable feast. One always got on very well and from the point of view of the Confederates the Valais was an "affiliated locality".

The last King of High Burgundy made the Bishop of Sion a present of the area in 999 on the upper reaches of the Rhone from the Furka to below the knee of the valley, the "Country Valais". On the passing of Burgundy into the Holy Roman Empire of German nations the cleric was awarded with all the insignia of worldly power and became an appointed Prince subject to the Emperor alone. In the course of the Centuries the bishops found better support from the people than from the nobles which was why they granted the farmers advisory rights as early as the 14th Century and introduced the Consilium generale terrae Vallesii, later the County Council. Self-conscious communes were formed such as that in Zermatt which on their part formed themselves into so-called "Zenden", that is, to independent republics. The individual "Zenden" (originally 7 and in the end 10) had their own Government, the "Zenden"-Council, their own banner and the right to conclude agreements abroad. Highest authority lay – in the overall state as well as in the "Zenden" – with the Communes. The state's form in the Valais was similar to that in ancient Switzerland but fully independent.

How can it be explained that in spite of all, Switzerland's form on the map is similar to a well-fed hedgehog squatting on the ground? Could it be that these sanctimonious Swiss are imperialists in disguise who one day set out to capture the run of the Rhone? Well, a normal extent of greediness is not to be denied to the hedgehog. With a healthy appetite he plunged into the gardens of his ducal neighbours when the necessity arose to safeguard his borders. Funnily enough, these simple men in their spiked disguise did not think of granting rights and freedom to the people in the occupied areas even if these were glad to rid themselves of their princely yoke. The Confederates established bailiffs and only called these back under the sound of the fanfares of the French Revolution. In the same manner the Upper Valaisans proceeded in the area of the Rhone estuary at the higher end of the Lake of Geneva where they were obliged to protect themselves against the quarrelsome Dukes of Savoy and only made room on the Council benches for their subjects in 1798. Thus it is explained why in the Valais one not always dances to the piper's tune.

The last morsel acquired by the hedgehog was at the time of the Vienna Congress – under the eyes of the Great Powers who distributed Napoleon's legacy, the Valais was given to fodder in 1815. The Valaisans had the choice

A lonely path in the Riffel woods, ideal of summer happiness, the dream of millions of people crammed in the great towns and cities. Does one not owe them the up-keep of the woods, and this in spite of clearing wide paths for ski runs?

of two evils, to slither into the dependancy of Paris as an independent republic or to break its way to the Confederation. Under the impression of the passing French guns and the news that Napoleon had escaped from Elba it was easy to decide for the welcome open arms extended by the Swiss. When, however, in 1848, the provisional Swiss Constitution was to be replaced by a better structure; from a Federation of States to a Confederation, the people in the Upper Valais voted so strongly against this, by 100:10, causing embarrassed silence in the new cantonal capital of Sion; the first Federal compromise was due: – One would submit in the Valais if the majority of the Swiss people and the cantons were for approval. The Constitution came into effect. We have already learnt of the effects.

The Visp-Zermatt railway was built in 1890 through the intermediary of Lausanne and Basle bankers.

The delight of all tourists: A herd of real Upper Valais blacknecked goats. One barely sees them anymore and if the Kurverein had not taken action this amusing animal would have vanished from the Zermatter scene like the cows.

Remotely Controlled Along the Vispe

No philosopher would make out a good testimonial for keeping technical developments in hand. Humanity has done everything wrong. It could, however, be that the inhabitants of Zermatt have also here danced out of tune with healthy intuition. Where the Zurichois, the Balois and the Bernese, Genevese and Lausannois break a tooth; on the limitation of individual traffic in favour of an increase in the standard of living, the people under the Matterhorn have already shown with success without any damage. Zermatt is free of motor vehicles, the cars remain 6 km below the village. Transport is effected by an efficient railway. It is not that progress is less appreciated here than elsewhere; in place of the little train that used to steam through the Nikolai valley with two-axled summer coaches six times a day, there is today a long composition which, remotely controlled, covers the line sixty times a day and this in half the time and right through the year. The idea, coveted by the inhabitants of Randa and Täsch, that if the railway was otherwise of not much use at least the steam engines could in an emergency be used as fire engines, had been thoroughly dissipated. In 1966 the Brig-Visp-Zermatt railway was the first Swiss private railway which had been provided on the whole line with centrally controlled supervision. With this, the base was laid for an increase in frequency, travelling speed and safety. In the train from Stalden, one leans out of the window to the right and out of the window to the left to be sure not to miss the first glimpse of the Matterhorn. One is at first little concerned with time-table or with safety and yet one will suddenly observe that in Kalpetran, in St. Niklaus, Herbriggen and Randa there is no redcapped man under the station roof to give the signal for the departure of the train. The train seems to set itself in motion uncontrolled.

There is no reason for worry: the train reserves its own line. On travelling over the last block-section of the line before the station, the entry and signals are prepared at the same time, the exit signal is cleared and the line is automatically pre-blocked.

Top: Straw bales are brought to the highest stables above Törbel by pack-horse. Törbel lies high above the gorge of the Vispe near Stalden and has today, as only village of the Nikolai valley, twenty well-kept pack-horses in the stables.

Bottom: In 1972 rye was still planted beyond Täsch. It was cut with a sickle. In the Zermatt area rye has completely vanished in the last years. The grain even ripened in Findelen at 2200 metres. See also the picture page 115.

If the line is already occupied by a train coming the other way (the whole line is single-tracked) the crossing automatically takes place in the station. Here we have to wait. If, however, another train is running in the same direction in front, then the exit signal clears the line itself as soon as the section is free. If the signals are open and the moment has come for departure according to the time-table, it only requires the check by the conductor that the last suitcase is loaded to give the signal to the engine-driver to continue. Once the train has passed two short current-circuits the block section is signalled open. Checking of the end of the train is eliminated because all vehicles are fitted with vacuum brakes and the loss of a carriage would automatically bring the train to an immediate stop.

*No. 1 Matterhorn, 2 Monte Rosa, 3 Mischabel, 4 Gornergrat, 5 St. Theodul, 6 Weisshorn, 7 Breithorn, 8 Lyskamm. "Breithorn" is still in operation for group travel, "Weisshorn" is in Chur. Nos. 2, 3, 5–8 were subsequently fitted with superheaters. 1929, Nos. 1–5 scrapped, 1935 No. 8.
** Rack-rail section/Adhesion section.   *** increased to 928 hp in 1945.

Crested carriages: No. 2041 Brig, No. 2042 Visp, No. 2043 Zermatt.

Abbreviations: – SLM Swiss Locomotive and Machine Works Winterthur, BBC Brown Boveri & Co., Baden; MFO Oerlikon Machine Works, SIG Swiss Industrial Society Neuhausen, SAAS Sécheron Geneva, SWS Swiss Coach Factory Schlieren.

Below: The Mühlebach bridge of the Brig-Visp-Zermatt railway between Stalden and Kalpetran. The Matter Vispe has dug a gorge 80 metres deep beneath the wooded valley slopes.

The Traction Vehicles of the Brig-Visp-Zermatt Railway (original state)

	Steam engines	Steam engines
Operating number *	1-6	7-8
Year of construction	1890-1902	1906-1908
Type and series	2/3 II	HG 2/3
Heating area, sq. m	64	63,5
Grate area, sq. m	1,26	1,25
Traction pinions	2	2
Water capacity in litres	2530	2500
Coal capacity in kg	1300	1300
Overall length in m	7624	7636
Service weight in tons	29	31,7
Constructor	SLM	SLM
Ascent and descent, km p.h. **	7/25	10/30
Loaded weight of train, tons	46	80
Capacity of train, seats	110	140
Type-illustration, page	113	

 1-8
 11-15
 16

	El. engine	El. engine	Dbl. mot.-coach	Dbl. mot.-coach
Operating number	11-15	16	2031-2032	2041-2043
Year of construction	1929-30	1939	1960	1965
Type and series	HGe 4/4	HGe 4/4	ABDhe 6/6	ABDhe 8/8
Driving motors	4	4	6	8
Traction pinions	4	4	6	8
Performance per hour, hp	800 ***	928	1200	1600
Overall length in m	14,1	14,2	32,3	36,1
Weight in tons	48	45	69	83
Constructor mech. part	SLM-SWS	SLM-SWS	SLM-SIG	SLM
Constructor elect. part	MFO	MFO	SAAS	SAAS
Ascent km per hour **	20/45	25/50	25/55	25/55
Loaded weight of train, tons	108	128	130	170
Capacity of train, seats	160	200	250	350
Type-illustration, page				54

2031-2032

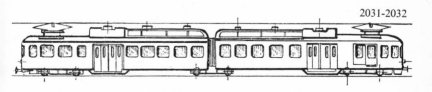

Control of the overall traffic is effected from the Domino-line-switch-desk which is situated in the administrative building of the Brig-Visp-Zermatt and Gornergrat railways in Brig (the two individually autonomous railways have an operational community with a common director). Thanks to the automatic line blocks and the remote control, one operator can supervise the whole traffic between Brig and Zermatt even if the small stations are not being serviced (picture page 52). By press-button control – always one key for the track and one key for the signal – it is possible to effect a crossing or overtaking manoeuvre, that is, to speed up a train and to hold up another. This, of course, only as long as the block section before the station is not occupied. Foolish orders are not carried out. Remote control transmission is effected by a double code and over an individual cable whose approximately 60 strands permits the simultaneous transmission of numerous messages. Green and red indicator lamps on the line-switch-desk continually

Left: The old pack-horse track to Zermatt leads sixty metres above the railway line on the sunny wasteland before coming to Kalpetran. The new road into the Nikolai valley cuts through the wood ravines on the opposite side without touching the hamlet. Above the pine-studded rock on the right is the village of Embd. In the steep slope underneath the grape still grows.

Below: In the V-formed gorge of Kipfen, river, railway, path and road are tightly packed above each other to find a way through. There has just been a thunderstorm: The narrow Vispe surges dirtily through the gorge. Since its water is being used for the generation of electricity it only carries about a quarter of its original quantity of water.

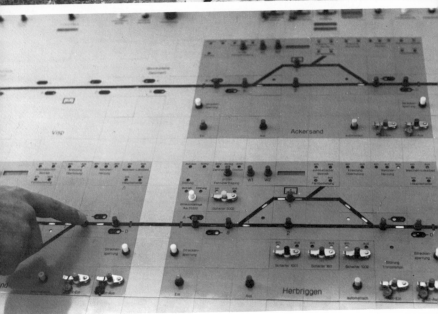

signal the actual conditions on the 44 km line. The plant comprises the main and overtaking track with heatable points on ten automatic crossing stations and eleven block points – these are connection points between the sections. On a darker area on the screen on the desk individual station installations can be seen. Block points are coordinated to their nearest station where also the relay apparatus are concentrated. A common supervisory relay

Line and Constructions of the Brig-Visp-Zermatt Railway

Present operational length	43 979 m
Length owned by company	43 396 m
Stations and stops	11
Maximum gradient of 12.5%	on 7 642 m i. e. cog-rail section 18%
2.5%	on 35 754 m, i. e. adhesion section 82%
Corners	on 7 172 m, i. e. 16% of overall length
Tunnels and galleries	16 with an overall length of 2 680 m of which 8 avalanche galleries with an overall length of 2 363 m; longest is 652 m
Bridges and viaducts	39 with a total length of 467 m, Mühlebach bridge has a length of 73 m
Crossing loops	71

Present Rolling Stock of the Brig-Visp-Zermatt Railway

Double motor coaches	5	Nos. 2031-2032, No. 2041 Brig, 2042 Visp, 2043 Zermatt
Electric engines	6	Nos. 11-16
Steam engines	1	No. 7 Breithorn
Diesel tractors	2	
Passenger carriages	51	A Nos. 2061-2067, 2071-2078, AB Nos. 2121-2122, 2124, 2161-63, B Nos. 2221-2226, 2261-2276, 2281-2286, BD Nos. 2291-2292
Goods trucks	86	of which 4 luggage vans with post compartment, 6 tank waggons, 3 Isotherm and 2 container trucks
Service vehicles	11	of which 1 snowplough
Motor buses	4	Nos. 2001-2003, 2005

Top; The avalanche gallery "Schusslaui" of the Brig-Visp-Zermatt railway shortly before Zermatt. Both sides of the valley are continually ravaged by dangerous avalanches, rock-falls and torrents. Safe communications require huge protective constructions. The road is not open to the public. To make the road safe for traffic would cost further millions.

Below: Since 1966 the railway to Zermatt is automatically remotely controlled from the terminal station in Brig. The line is divided into eleven blocks. Per day there are approximately 50 regular and 10 special trains and in addition twenty shuttle trains between Täsch and Zermatt.

signals failures to the remote control as well as to the switch desk in the station itself.

If individual operation is requested by a station in order to carry out a manoeuvre, automatic control can be switched off. Permanently operated stations by an official are only Brig, Visp and Zermatt. The stations are also shown on the line-switch-desk but only indicatively with the signals for entry and exit as well as the centralised block points. Installations for the operation of the signals in Visp are fitted in the Domino switchdesk of the Federal railways.

Incidentally; if you take the train to Zermatt, no matter which side of the carriage you sit you are in the right place. The view is exciting both to the left and to the right. The Matterhorn does not show itself at all until the last corner of the line. Or perhaps, yes – the Hörnli occasionally deigns to a greeting and claims the honour to be called the Matterhorn by the 'know-alls'.

The double motor-coach ABDhe 8/8 "Visp", built in 1965, one of the strongest vehicles of the Brig-Visp-Zermatt railway. Each half of the coach is an electric unit: it has a pantograph and four serially switched motors. All eight axles of the motor-coach are fitted with a permanently coupled unit for adhesion and cog-rail drive. – The neglected fields behind the station demonstrate the agricultural breakdown in Zermatt.

Pushing and Pulling

During the eighties of the last Century, Zermatt had been chosen as the playground for railway constructors. Central Switzerland and the Bernese Oberland had been milked dry and now the ripe fruit in the Valais was to be picked. To whom the idea of the "Zermatt high alpine railways" is to be credited, remains unclear. Various people claim the honour. But it was Caspar Leonhard Heer-Bétrix who presented it ready cast to the public. A railway can be one way or another. It grows from individual parts, from a frame of mind or a mood, knowledge and expertise, of coincidences and considerations, of old and of new. The birth can be a normal one – this one was a twin birth with complications.

Of Heer, railway history only says that he was a printer, the typographers add that truly he had a printing works in Bienne but he principally concerned himself with railways. The talented man's letterheading – the papers are in the Federal Archives – give, according to the circumstances, only very brief information on his activity. "Building" it says under the name. There is no doubt that the building expert was a friend of the mountains and a clever manager who, once having made a plan also put it diligently into practise. He knew nothing of "one should" – he was a man of decision. The formulation and lay-out of his concession application of 22. August 1890 bears witness to his careful management.

Heer must certainly also in Zermatt have come across the opinion that a railway must be built to the Gornergrat. It may, however, be presumed that he was the initiator for the Matterhorn railway and himself became the pushed. If at that period there did not exist a debating club for leading engineers and building experts, they certainly all periodically met in the entrance to the Federal Palace where they held the door for each other. Each one had a couple of concession applications in his pocket. Heer, in September of 1889, for the crossing of the Kleine Scheidegg in the Bernese Oberland (Wengernalp railway). Already four weeks following the publication he was to learn that his fine project threatened to be suffocated in the general excitement over two other applications which concerned a railway from the same village: the aim was the summit of the Jungfrau. Koechlin and Trautweiler were the two spoil-sports, a Zurichois and an Argovien. The one was the designer of the Eiffel Tower in Paris and the other an engineer with the Jura-Brunig railways. It was to be expected of both of them that they would place their planned funiculars with the same energy and expertise on the Matterhorn! If Heer was to ensure himself of priority in Zermatt, and from his experience and extensive surveys this was his fixed intention, then he

X.Jmfeld, Jngen.
à Berne

HAU

1	Adlerpass height, m	3789	13 Fee, Saas	m 1798	21 Liskamm	m 4527
2	Allalinhorn	4027	14 Ferpècle	1770	22 Matterhorn	4477
3	Alphubel	4206	Findelen	2051	23 Chli Matterhorn	3883
4	Bösentrift	3248	Fluhalp	2618	24 Mattmark	2120
5	Breuil-Cervinia	2006	15 Gabelhorn, Ober	4063	25 Mettelhorn	3406
6	Breithorn	4164	Unter	3391	26 Mont Miné	2914
7	Cima di Jazzi	3803	Gandegghütte	3029	Monte Rosa:	
8	Colle delle Loccie	3334	16 Glac. Durand		27 Dufourspitze	4634
9	Col d'Hérens	3462	17 Glac. Moiry		Nordend	4609
10	Dent Blanche	4357	18 Gornergrat	3135	Monte Rosahütte	2795
11	Dent d'Hérens	4171	19 Grand Cornier	3961	28 Mountethütte	2886
12	Dom	4545	20 Hörnli	2888	29 Randa	1439

56

RELIEF DES
ONTAGNES DE ZERMATT.

30	Riffelberg height, m	2566	39	Stockji	m 3091	47	Zermatt	m 1616
31	Riffelalp	2222	40	Strahlhorn	4190		Zmutt	1936
32	Riffelhorn	2927	41	Tête Blanche	3724	48	Zumsteinspitze	4563
33	Rimpfischhorn	4199	42	Theodulpass	3290		Zwillinge:	
34	Rothorn, Zinal	4221	43	Täschhorn	4490	49	Castor	4228
35	, Ober	3415		Trift	2337	50	Pollux	4092
36	, Unter	3103	44	Triftjoch	3530			
	Rothornhütte	3200		Triftthorn	3728		A plaster cast of the Zermatt	
37	Saas Grund	1559	45	Weisshorn	4505		high alpine relief by X. Im-	
	Schönbielhütte	2694		Weisshornhütte	2932		feld was a popular object	
	Schwarzsee	2583	46	Weisstor, Schwarzb.	3577		of demonstration around	
38	Stockhorn	3532		Wellenkuppe	3903		1880 and cost SFr. 2 300!	

would have to include the Matterhorn in the Gornergrat railway whether he wanted to or not.

Much time was not to be lost but Heer had made sure to appoint good assistants. Two months after he had been granted the concession of the Wengernalp railway by Parliament, the completed concession application for the Zermatter railways was ready. One was not pernickety with the tunnel railway on the Matterhorn. Koechlin and Trautweiler had planned four to five sections to overcome the 3300 metres difference in height on the Jungfrau project, Heer boldly put the 1350 metres difference in height between Whymper's hut and Matterhorn summit into one section. The lower part of the Matterhorn railway and the Gornergrat railway had, to be honest, the same pattern as the Wengernalp project – funicular on the wooded steep slope and subsequently a narrow-gauge rack-and-pinion electric railway. Clever, however, was the junction of the two tracks of Gornergrat and Matterhorn with the valley railway at "Gorge", at the entrance to the Gorneren gorge. Sensational for that period was the electric traction. (The first electric tram ran in 1891. Adhesion railways did not follow until 1899, eight years later.)

The whole manner in which the railway business was tackled – bringing it in from outside, not developing out of the Commune – caused displeaure among the highlanders. One could, however, speak one's mind and was heard, for after all, one was in free Switzerland. In a motion the Commune of Zermatt raised objection to the planned project. Also the inhabitants of Randa, Täsch, guides and porters took to the pen. They were worried about a possible decrease of their incomes.

In the Federal Palace one had immediately packed up the explosive papers of the concession applications and returned them to the Government at Sion with a request for comment. A great deal, it appeared. It was only a nuisance that the Zermatters would not agree and utterly unacceptable if the railways were not built by a Valais company.

This was easy to arrange: within a fortnight the head of the Federal Department of Railways received a second application. This could consider the, in the meantime, newly propagated pneumatic tunnel railway by Locher for the section of the Matterhorn. The letter said if the signatories had not previously requested the concession for both railways, then only because the opposition of the Zermatt inhabitants and private interests had hindered them to do so. Since the question was raised, however, one requested the granting of the concession. To keep distance from the first project was difficult. The topographer Xaver Imfeld, who knew the Matterhorn and the Gornergrat as no other, had refused his cooperation for – as he said – reasons of overwork. He was charged with topographic surveys of different railways.

Roman Abt's steam locomotives, as they were also used on the Visp-Zermatt line. For the first time they had an individual drive for cog-rail and adhesion sections. The cog wheels T1 and T2 with brake drums b1 and b2 are arranged in the inner frame supported by the running axles and are driven by two individual cylinders. As long as the running wheels do not leave their rails the cog grip remains safe. The two steam cylinders placed externally to the frame, drive the three running axles.

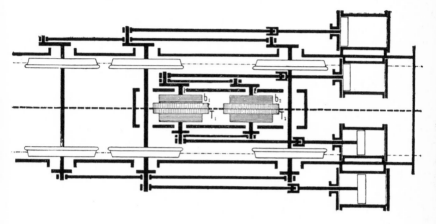

In 1885 Abt carried out the first tests on the Harz railway in Braunschweig with his new system. By distributing the cog grip on to a multipart cog wheel it was possible to provide the locomotive with smaller cog wheels and greater speed. The meshing junction of the cog wheels (below) consists of a longer cog-rail piece which, lengthwise pivotable, is held on flexible supports and thus connected with the fixed cog rails.

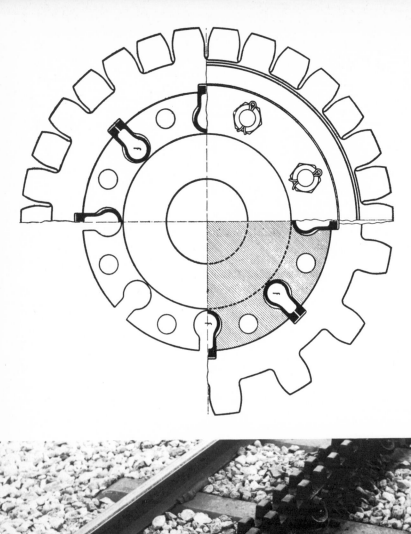

Like the Brig-Visp-Zermatt railway the Gornergrat railway, opened in 1898, is also based on the cog-rail system by Abt. It is, however, a pure cog-wheel drive and from the beginning was operated electrically. The illustration below shows the drive dispositions of the first engines He 2/2. It shows two running axles of which each one has its own drive. From the motor the 800 r.p.m. are transmitted with a first gear on to the shaft U-U. A second pair of gear wheels V transmit the movement to the axle on which the driving cog wheel T, with a diameter of 573 mm runs in the cog rail. On this axle are also fitted the brake drums b. Overall gear ratio 1:12.

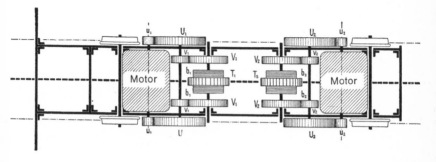

Left: Cog wheel and its double cog rail of the Gornergrat railway, system Abt. As the wheel consists of two discs with staggered teeth, several teeth simultaneously fit into the cog rail. Two cog wheels of the driving coach are so arranged that the intervals are even shorter. The tooth division of a cog wheel and the cog rail amounts to 120 mm as against the usual 100 mm with the Riggenbach system. The two discs of a cog wheel are fixed with bolts which are sprung within the boring. They take up division faults and provide safety and quiet running of the machine. The cog rail is fixed on sleepers.

Now the ball was in the court of the Zermatters. What did they have to say to a project whose leaders sat in Sion? They did still not like it but one had become realistic; in a meeting of 16. November 1890 the Communal Council decided to request for time and to put in an application for concession for the Gornergrat railway themselves. They would be glad to leave the Matterhorn with its immense problems of technical, physical and physiological nature to other future concessionaries and to the Federal authorities. Time – one had in mind a period of five years until the completion of the detailed plans for the Gornergrat railway – this was necessary because adaption to the altered conditions had to be made possible for the guides, porters and saddle-horse operators. In addition the Visp-Zermatt railway was still under construction. Besides the signatures of the elected burghers' representatives, the clever motion was also signed by Alexander Seiler, the inn proprietor and master over 600 hotel beds.

Hands were raised to heaven in the High Council in Sion. "Gentlemen, please agree" one member warned "it could otherwise happen that we are obliged to vote for an outside project!" The Cantonal surveyor, Zen Ruffinen

The cog-rail points are complicated. Left: One of the seven heated spring-points of the Gornergrat railway at Riffelberg station. The points are set from the switch desk in the station or automatically by the train which is coming in if the section is not blocked.

Right: The original points at the time of construction at Kulm station. The two cog rails are individually arranged in the junction and run directly up to the rail so that the cog wheel is continually in contact. The air-operated points on three-phase operating railways are also complicated.

and National Councillor Roten invited Zermatt to participate in their project with equal rights and to make the pie tasty, they for the moment waived the realisation of the Matterhorn railway.

There was no reply. What had happened? Something tragic and extraordinary at the same time.

While an opinion was being sought in the Valais, Leonhard Heer had to undergo an operation. On 12. December 1890 he informed the Federal Council that his interests would be looked after by engineer Xaver Imfeld during his absence, "who had also been present during the preliminary work on the project and participated with equal rights on the concession". The letter was accompanied with their financial agreement with the Federal Bank in Bern. From this it is seen that this bank agreed to the financing of this matter if it proved to be possible to carry out. A few days later Heer died. Imfeld had already in the spring of 1890 concluded agreements with Leonhard Heer with the purpose of realising three different railway projects among which the Zermatter railways. He now was the speaker for the application and with Imfeld being involved, the situation completely changed.

There are no records available that there was sufficient wine in the village in order to keep tongues wetted in the discussion over the new position of the matter. There are records, however, that everyone must have known Imfeld. Since 14 years he had moved up and down the valley like a native. Had one not dunked bread in one's milk together in the hut and trodden every mountain path with this humble and humorous man. He knows every step and every rock, the run of every water and the paths of the avalanches. And – his wife is from Zermatt. Xaver Imfeld came from Sarnen in Obwalden, his picture hangs in the Alpine Museum in Bern with the legend: – "1853–1909, a topographer of genius". Following his education at the Federal Polytechnicum he was sent on behalf of the Federal Topographical Office to the Valais to bring the National Map in the scale of 1:50 000 by Dufour up to date and to adapt it for the new Siegfried Atlas. To his pen is due the truly excellent reproduction of the natural rock and contours in 21 high alpine map sheets. He was awarded many honours.

Imfeld may be considered as the promoter of the project of the Gornergrat railway. Already in 1886 when he was carrying out topographic surveys for the Visp-Zermatt railway he had recognised the necessary extension on the Gornergrat and had reconnoitred the area. Together with the responsible technical engineer of the project Heer he had undertaken ground studies for the preparation of the plans and had studied the available water power

Other Railways in the Rhone Valley

Railways	Inau-gurated	Type	Gauge cm	Length km	Steepest gradient %	Original power system
Bex-Villars-Bretaye	1898	AR Abt	100	17,1	20	E
Aigle-Leysin	1900	AR Abt	100	6,2	20	E
Aigle-Sépey-Diablerets	1905	A	100	22,4	6	E
Martigny-Châtelard	1906	AR Strub	100	20,9	10	E
Simplon (Tunnel)	1906	A	143,5	(19,8)	2,7	SE *
Aigle-Ollon-Monthey-Champéry	1907	AR Strub	100	23,1	13,5	E
Martigny-Orsières	1910	A	143,5	25,7	4	E
Sierre-Montana-Crans	1911	F	100	4,3	48,4	E
Lötschberg (Tunnel)	1913	A	143,5	(14,6)	2,7	E
Furka-Oberalp	1914-26	AR Abt	100	100,4	11	S **
Leuk-Leukerbad ***	1915	AR Abt	100	10,2	16	E
Châtelard-Barberine	1948	F	100	1,3	87	E

A Adhesion, R Rack-rail, F Funicular, E Electricity, S Steam.

* The first electric trials were unsatisfactory.

** Electrified in 1941; *** Closed in 1967.

and visitor frequency in Zermatt. Because he did not wish to draw his wife's family into the expected difficulties, he had asked Leonhard Heer to keep his name secret for the time being.

In May 1891 the Commune of Zermatt advised Bern and Sion that they supported the project Imfeld-Heer and waived the right of submission for their own plans for the Gornergrat railway. Imfeld and the Heer legatees, wife and son, had cleared the details of the ceding of ground with the Burghers' Council, and had agreed to the move of the headquarters of the company to Sion and the appointment of a cantonal representative to the Board of Directors. Thus the demands were fulfilled which were made by the Valais State Council. In accordance to the Federal Department of Railways the petitioners had agreed to bring the required proof of safety for their 3000 metre fourth section of the Matterhorn railway and to actively and financially assist the tests being made by Koechlin for the Jungfrau railway. It was considered only fair by the Federal Palace that not only one should bear the high cost if the investigations were to the benefit of both. "And that too," the authors of the project in Sion may have sighed. They, who after the refusal by Zermatt had about-faced to the full plan now finally renounced. The Federal Parliament in their meeting of 20. June 1892 gave their agreement to the last existing application for concession, Imfeld-Heer.

The concession was granted at a time of growing distrust of mountain railways. In 1893 there were no less than 92 railway concessions for new lines in Switzerland which were not yet under construction. Under such conditions who wanted to invest money in a Matterhorn railway? Drop it, advised the bank. Precious money. Had anyone asked where it came from? No one appeared to find objection to the interesting fact that the banks supporting the competing petitioners were all in Bern in the same street!

But not only the financing provided difficulties, no, also the motivation of the Matterhorn railway. Protests came from all sides. Mountaineers, naturalists, doctors, Zermatters, Swiss and foreigners announced their misgivings. The shadow of the mountain lay crushing and paralysing over the railway project. In 1894 the concessionaires requested an extension of the time for submission of the technical and financial detailed plans as well as of the statutes of the company to be formed. The knot now had to be cut. The Federal Parliament decided in favour of an extension on behalf of the Gornergrat railway – because at present only this had lapsed – and declared with emphasis, the lapse of the one did not necessarily follow in the cancelling of the other line. When the term for the extension of the Matterhorn railway became due, Parliament declined its support. Since then the Matterhorn again belongs to the mountaineers without limitations.

The struggle for the concession and the financing had given the Gornergrat railway time to develop into one of the most beautiful Swiss railways. Thanks

The starter resistor of the first Gornergrat railway engine for two three-phase motors.

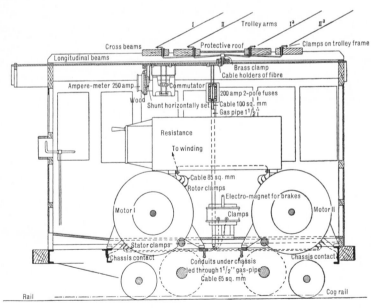

Trolley arms

I   II   I^a   II^a

Cross beams   Protective roof   Clamps on trolley frame

Longitudinal beams

Brass clamp
Cable holders of fibre

Ampere-meter 250 amp.   Commutator

Wood   200 amp 2-pole fuses

Shunt horizontally set   Cable 100 sq. mm

Gas pipe 1½''

Resistance

To winding

Cable 85 sq. mm

Rotor clamps

Electro-magnet for brakes

Motor I   Clamps   Motor II

Stator clamps

Chassis contact   Chassis contact

Conduits under chassis
led through 1½'' gas-pipe
Cable 65 sq. mm

Rail   Cog rail

to new technical developments it could now be risked to extend electric cog-and-pinion operation through the steep Riffelwald right down next to the station of the Visp-Zermatt railway. The joint stock company was founded on 11. June 1896. The cost of the railway amounted to SF 3 million.

Left: The Rowan train No. 1 of the Gornergrat railway in the year 1898. Rowan was constructor of the locomotive which is connected to the two coaches, similarly to a horse, by two extending iron beams so that the weight of the passenger coach helps to put extra load on the two driving wheels. The attached coach only has one axle. The train carried 110 passengers. With pure rack railways the locomotive must always be on the lower end of the train on the ascent as well as on the descent. This is to avoid that a passenger carriage can become loose and travel on its own.

Diagrams: The three-phase locomotives He 2/2 of the Gornergrat railway, built together with those of the Jungfrau railway, were the first electric rack-rail locomotives in Switzerland. The two 40-cycle asynchronous motors of 90 hp developed a pulling power of 6000 kg at 500 Volt operating current. Average driving speed amounted to 7.2 kilometres per hour.

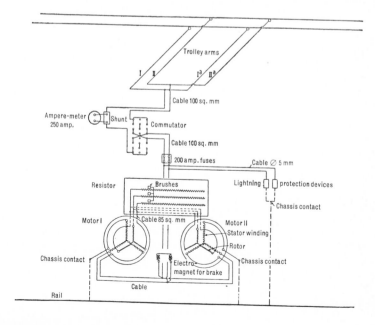

The Trick with the Current

The world could not imagine a more beautiful area than the Gornergrat for the first trial with a three-phase current operated locomotive. The great day was 24. November 1897. While 7000 horses of the City tram trotted through the streets of Berlin, one was occupied in Zermatt with unloading a heavy motor-coach from the goods wagon of the Visp-Zermatt railway and to put in on the first 2 kilometres of the completed section of the Gornergrat railway. The normal composition was already available as a test train: an articulated locomotive connected to the passenger carriage. This construction provided the advantage against other separated vehicles of greater operational safety. The motor-coach – that is the fixed connection of driving vehicle and passenger compartments – was lighter and more stable but at the same time put a greater load on the cog wheel and thus had a better braking effect. The two-axle cog-wheel driving frame supported the separate coach body of the locomotive with two motors, the required cog transmission and the brakes

Rowan train No. 4, 1902. The feature of this three-phase operation are the two overhead lines and the two two-pole trolleys. Current-return is effected through the rail. At the side of the rails the three wires of the parallel supply line are suspended. A 30 cm high metalling forms the 360 cm wide rail-bed which is supported by side rock walling. The gauge is 100 cm, maximum gradient 20%.

while the frame for the passenger coach rested at its top end on a two-axle bogie, the lower end was supported by extending beams, universibly mobile, on the frame of the engine. The two engine motors were three-phase alternating current induction motors of 90 hp.

The representatives of industry and the builders as well as the invited officials and the press were more than satisfied with the new-born child, having shown that even with maximum load of 28.5 tons it had no trouble in travelling up the incline of the Outer Woods at the planned speed of 7 km per hour. The speed was maintained on the horizontal as well as on gradients without the engine driver having to do anything to the switchgear. Praise ran high on the quiet and regular descent. With unengaged brakes the train soon reached its normal speed of 7 km and never exceeded this! There were only raised eyebrows on the trolleys, those four contact rollers which connect the engine with the overhead line. On switching over of the engine these required time-consuming manoeuvres and were therefore replaced by contact shoes. A duplicate arrangement of the trolleys, however, proved to be necessary in order to avoid current interruptions on crossing points and

The Findelenbach power station of the Gornergrat railway around the turn of the century. The turbine plant consists of three Girard high pressure turbines of 250 hp and Brown Boveri three-phase generators. Three transformers at kilometres 2, 5 and 8 reduce the primary current of 5400 Volts to 540 Volts. The water drop in the pipe-line amounted to 107 metres. In summer 15 000 litres and winter 3500 litres per second were measured.

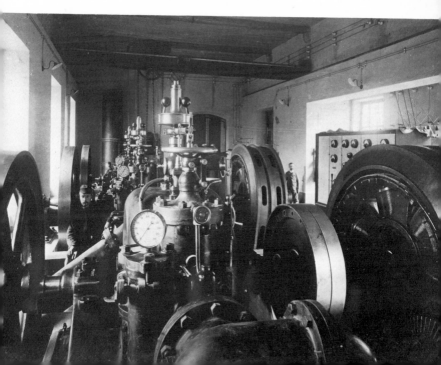

overhead line junctions. The secret of the regular running of the three-phase engine consists in that the motors act as generators on the descent and return the excess energy into the overhead line.

The same newspapers which had informed the Berliners on the number of horses gave an extensive description of the test on the Gornergrat. The 5400 volt three-phase current produced in the power station, it said, is reduced to 540 volts of the operational power. Two conductors in the form of 8.5 mm copper wire are suspended at a height of 4 metres above the centre of the rails and the rails themselves serve as third conductor. The imagination that 244 horse-drawn trams depart in all direction per hour from the Potsdamer Platz today clearly equally belongs to the world of legend as the idea at that time to travel up a mountain with an electric railway and to return in one piece.

The Swiss electrotechnical industry was leading in the field of development of electric railways. This was no coincidence. On the 3000 km of track which the country had eighty years ago, only steam operated trains circulated. The fuel had to be imported from far away; for the Swiss coal supplies barely sufficed for the heating of a stove to warm cold hands. Water, however, flows from all the mountains. The only difficulty was to distribute the obtained electric power over long distances. This required high voltages as otherwise the conductors became too thick, heavy and expensive. The Oerlikon Machine Works had since 1890 a test plant with over 100 insulators in operation with which they proved for the first time that it was possible to transmit high current over long distances and to build transformers which besides absolute operational safety could provide a favourable service effect. The engineer C.E.L. Brown who for some time had concerned himself with multiple phase current had created the three-phase motor. It was suited to the characteristic features of the transmission system. The transformers permitted to keep the primary voltage as low as required, three-phase current on the other hand, can be easily transformed and the motor is simple. 1895 – Brown had in the meantime got together with Walter Boveri – the first test runs of their mutually developed tram driven by direct three-phase current took place between Lugano and Paradiso. It was to set the example for the Gornergrat engine and thus for the first electric cog-wheel locomotive in Switzerland.

Crane and Bulldozer - A Wish

The Zermatt schoolmaster certainly could not resist to give his pupils an essay as homework on the test runs in the Outer Woods before Christmas. The railway had begun to win the hearts of the Zermatters. Unfortunately, the engine did not also bring electric light to the village. At the beginning of the nineties Zermatt, as first mountain village in the Valais, had built its own power station. Most of the boys and girls, however, will probably still have had to move their tables to the windows in order to write the essay in the light of the lantern in the street for electric light was still beyond the means of many families. Naturally the power station at the Triftbach was not sufficient to supply the Gornergrat railway with power as well as the hotels. The former had to build its own. One would imagine that prior to the first sod to be turned, the Gornergrat Company had been founded; but this

Line and Constructions of the Gornergrat Railway

Present operational length	9 339 m of which 2 534 m double track
Stations and stops	7
Maximum gradient of 20%	on 5 200 m length, i.e. 56% of total length
Corners	on 3 089 m length, i.e. 32% of total length
Tunnels and galleries	5 with a total length of 1 320 m of which loop-tunnel 174 m, avalanche gallery Riffelbord 720 m
Bridges and viaducts	5 with a total length of 127 m. Vispe bridge 24 m, Findelenbach bridge 90 m and 50 m high
Crossing loops	30

was not the case: – the workers moved out in the middle of May 1896 and the company was formed on 11. June after the capital of SF 2 million (4000 bearer shares at SF 500) and the debenture loan of SF 1.5 million (1500 debentures at SF 1000) had been subscribed. A group of banks in Zurich, Basle and Bern dealt with the public subscription and agreed to take over whatever part was not subscribed by third parties. As with most railways, setting up of the project, construction and operation lay in different hands. Usually, for easier financing, the installation was built on contract and following its

Zermatt at the time of the construction of the Gornergrat railway, 1897. The works locomotive on the Visp bridge transports material over the completed section to the higher sites. The electric overhead line is still missing. In the foreground of the village the "Viehgasse" or cattle track, behind it the three big hotels, Zermatterhof, Monte Rosa and Mont Cervin. Zermatt already has over 800 hotel beds and 15 000 guests per summer.

→

conclusion taken over lock, stock and barrel by the railway company. This was also the case with the Gornergrat railway. The builders, Haag & Greulich of Bienne agreed with the consortium of banks and the future company to construct the railway at fixed conditions. Simultaneously the concessionaires were to cede their rights to the railway company. Haag & Greulich's specifications laid down final project and construction of the railway including power station and electrical installations, purchase of land and water rights as well as the purchase of rolling stock and ancillary equipment for an all-inclusive sum of SF 3 million. The railway was to be completely equipped and ready for operation on 1. July 1898. Each day's delay was subject to a penalty of SF 2000. If, in spite of this, Mr. Greulich who was to manage project and construction, was still able to sleep following the signing of the contract, it was because of his extensive technical experience in railway construction. He was a man of brilliant mental flexibility which permitted him to find solutions which were not available in any textbook. On 20. August 1898 the Gornergrat railway was ceremoniously inaugurated. There had been no lack of surprises during the time of construction. Apart from the extraordinarily wet first summer, the unexpected prohibition of night blasting by

An Abt II/3 rack-rail tender locomotive, originally intended for Aix-les-Bains, it served the Gornergrat railway as an additional locomotive. In 1920 it was sold to Montserrat in Spain. The long boiler is mounted at an angle so that the water level always remains above the boiler-pipes on the steep gradient of the climb.

the Canton and early snowfall added to the problems. For the completion of the Findelen stream bridge an emergency solution had to be found because there was too little time to mason the round arches. There were furthermore extremely hard rock parts where 30 drills were necessary to drill a hole of 35 cm depth. Mountain sickness lurked in wait of victims. After several weeks at 2700 metres above sea level the efficiency of the workers attained its normal limits, at 3000 metres, efficiency dropped to nil. In order to pierce all the tunnels and complete those lower down during the winter of 1896/97, 150 men had to be accommodated in barracks at the Riffelalp. All went well. In the following summer the accommodation was moved up to the Rotenboden. At this point mountain sickness set in after the beginning of the cool weather with influenza-type symptoms and the railway doctor had to order the withdrawal of the whole team.

Xaver Imfeld no longer took part in the detailed surveys and planning. His work on his now famous Montblanc map in the scale of 1:50 000 had overtaxed his health. Contrary to his desire, he found himself unable to carry out the levelling for the Gornergrat railway himself. On 30. January 1894 after having taken the project through all the negotiating phases with contagious enthou-

On the slopes threatened by avalanches and snow pressure, the overhead line had to be removed in the autumn and rebuilt in the spring. A wooden construction which was pushed by the steam locomotive on a goods truck served as fitting platform. The re-opening in the spring was always a race with the calendar.

siasm he relinquished his concession participation to August Haag, an architect who like the Heer family, lived at the foot of the Jura. It was to be expected that one had turned to Haag because he was already together with the late Heer on numerous railway projects in the Bernese Oberland. Also there, August Haag had constructed under contract together with a partner. For the Gornergrat railway he went into partnership with the extremely clever Karl Greulich of Lucerne, a railway engineer reknowned beyond the frontier.

The most difficult problem was to find a solution to overcome the ramp between Zermatt and Riffelalp. Besides two large bridges a chain of tunnels and supporting walls were required. The originally intended mixed operation by adhesion, cable and cog rail was dropped in favour of a direct electric

The construction of the Findelenbach bridge at kilometer 1.9 and in a gradient of 12.4% was started in 1896. In the first summer only the foundations had been laid and the lower pilon built up to 15 metres. In view of the lack of time in the third summer, the planned stone arches had to be given up and a steel framework fitted on to the pilons.

76

rack-and-pinion railway throughout. The Federal Department of Railways had approved the new plans on 1. April 1896. In justification it must also be said why Leonhard Heer expected his passengers to put up with the repeated complicated changing of transport. Simply because industry could not promise him a strong electric rack-and-pinion locomotive and no safe overhead line! The printer, however, must have been able to read better between the lines in the book of technical development than many of his contemporaries. He stubbornly kept to electric traction and accepted the electric operated funicular with a simpler construction for the steep incline.

Two things are required for a rack-and-pinion railway: – Rolling stock and its suitable track. To fit both together and to find the combination which, besides the highest safety of the trains, permits the cheapest way of construction and operation is probably the most important task of the engineers. Operational economy demands a lowest possible incline as operational costs disproportionately increase with growing gradient. Instead of packing all people into one train it would be necessary to run twice on a steep section. The line of the Gornergrat railway is very regularly laid, the highest gradient of not more than 20% (at an average incline of 16%) permitted the use of large vehicles from the start. The list of requirements of the rack-and-pinion railway, however, is longer: – In view of the special construction of the safety brakes, reverse down-gradients must be avoided, steep ramps should

The strength of the 50 metre high Findelenbach bridge is regularly checked.

be straight and high embankments are undesirable because the settling of the ground can lead to irregularities in the cog-guide.

The power station near the bridge at the Findelen stream was designed fully to the requirements of the railway. With a train weight of 28 tons, an incline

Travelling Times of the Gornergrat Railway and the Visp-Zermatt Trains

in minutes		Steam engines	Electric engines previously	Motor-coaches today
Zermatt - Gornergrat	Ascent		80	40
	Descent		80	40
Visp - Zermatt	Ascent	153	89	65
	Descent	138	93	68

of 20% and a speed of 2 metres per second, 160 hp were required. If the unavoidable transmission loss is added, a performance in the power station of 255 hp per train with 110 passengers is arrived at. It follows that with the three installed machine units of 250 hp each, simultaneously two fully loaded trains could be run uphill and one train downhill and one unit was still left as reserve. At the time of the electrification of the Visp-Zermatt railway a parallel was established between the power station Findelenbach and the network of the Swiss Federal railways and at the same time the generation of power for the Gornergrat railway was adapted to 50 cycle operation. Today most of the water of the Findelen stream is largely collected at the mouth of the glacier and fed into the dam of the Grande Dixence. The Gornergrat railway which in any case requires more power than the station can produce, is dependent on outside power.

Each of the two pantographs of the motor-coach is supplied from the overhead line with two current phases. The third phase is permanently connected to the rails by earth brushes. The overhead line current should lie between 650 and 800 volts. Two transformers in the terminal stations and five along the line provide for the supply of the network. A further supply line runs parallel to the overhead line which hops along the masts at a count of three: – At the first mast it supplies the first phase to the overhead line, at the second mast the second phase and at the third mast it bends down and supplies the third phase into the rail.

Snowploughing

Even in August and in the shade of a cool fanning larch, the idea of a "schuss" over soft, crystal-like glimmering slopes in the sunlight drive one to frenzy. Skiing is a passion: – only the thought of it and your feet come together, the hands grasp the sticks, hips sway in the rythm of the turns, eyes sparkle. Snowdust flies from the skis – faster, faster . . . . .

So what? Neither does the Gornergrat railway lose its breath. The rotary snowploughs turn their mighty shovels, throwing the snow well-aimed out over the track, the spikes grind into the compact mass, hack, cut and tear whatever is in the way. Faster, faster! Are 370 revolutions per minute not enough? Two mighty electric rotary snowploughs keep the line opened for the unremittingly circulating motor-coaches after the heaviest snowfall and storms of nature in a very short time. The little snowplough cleans up and removes remains of ice and snow from the cog rail. The Gornergrat railway was built for the summer and has its peak in winter. Again millions of francs had to be pumped into the undertaking in order to safeguard the track. This time, public authorities assisted because the railway had proved its importance for the development of the region. The great enemy of winter traffic in the mountains are the avalanches. It is not a coincidence that there is a small indicator lamp on the control desk of the Brig-Visp-Zermatt railway which warns of avalanche cover. In the 1920's the only connection with

Zermatt was by the post-sled drawn by a pack-horse. From November until May the railway between St. Niklaus and Zermatt was closed down. Only in 1933, following extensive protective constructions, full-year operation could be taken up. At the same period the Gornergrat railway put their snow-

Present Rolling Stock of the Gornergrat Railway

Double motor-coaches	4	Bhe 4/8 Nos. 3041-3044
Single motor-coaches	12	Bhe 2/4 Nos. 3011-3022
Electric engines	3	He 2/2 Nos. 3001-3003
Passenger carriages	none	
Goods trucks	4	of which 1 water-tank truck
Service vehicles	4	of which 2 rotary snowploughs, 1 snowplough and 1 fitters truck

plough into action in order to open the line as far as Riffelalp. Later, one dared go as far as Riffelboden and shortly following the second World War and the completion of the avalanche gallery at the Riffelbord the great break-through of skiing on the Gornergrat started. The long band of the gallery can be seen right down to Randa. Hidden away are some hundred metres of protective railing and retaining walls which are systematically arranged high up in the 40° flank above and below the Riffelalp in order to protect from snow drifts and slides. Together with these constructions, large areas of slopes were planted with trees. A healthy forest and continual supervision of possible avalanche areas during the critical time are still the best protection from damage even if the descent of unexpected avalanches can be prevented by artificial blasting.

With a performance of 2 x 180 hp the rotary snow-plough X rot e No. 3932, built in 1969, removes the masses of snow from the rails of the Gornergrat railway. The coach body and the plough itself can be swivelled by 360 degrees on the chassis. The vehicle must be moved by a pusher engine.

Overleaf: The avalanche gallery Riffelbord has a length of 720 m. In the winter the sides facing the valley are closed by wooden boarding. Numerous protective constructions along the line today safeguard unhindered traffic.

→

Motor-Coaches on Double Track

Taking one of the brown sun-baked Rowan trains with double rack driving cogs and double trolley onto the track and bearing in mind modern mass tourism, it takes little imagination to visualise the picture of the orange-coloured, 30 metre long motor-coach of the Gornergrat railway. The motor-coach is the logical further development of the Rowan train. In order to carry even less dead weight, that is in other words, to increase driving speed, the driving locomotive and passenger carriage were simply united under one roof. The double motor-coach is made up of two single motor-coaches with the only difference that it only has two driving cabins and two pantographs. It therefore has a correspondingly larger passenger capacity. A Rowan train with coach carried 110 people with a speed of 7.2 km per hour. The single motor-coach also carries 110 passengers but now with a speed of 14.5 km per hour. The double motor-coach has a capacity of 230 passengers. The next step would be a coupling of two double motor-coach trains. (Pictures pages 66, 85 and 89, table page 87).

A double motor-coach and single coach of the Gornergrat railway are ready in Zermatt station to take skiers to the snow slopes of the Riffelberg. Already in the station hall passengers are grouped according to space available in the waiting trains to avoid crowding.

From whichever point it is regarded, the cog railway is the most rational and modern means of transport in the mountains. There is no other which is capable of moving packets of over 200 tourists to the heights in short periods. In addition, the cog railway is operationally reliable, does not take up unnecessary space, is quiet and on top of it all causes no pollution. It must also be agreed that the cog railway, in spite of its considerable age has not been put on a side-line by industry. On the contrary. It has at its disposal modern equipment to justify at any time the requirements of the mountain railways. Even for the production of rack-rails there exist highly modern automatic machines. Electrically operated points are supplied, and remote-controlled train compositions with a high degree of comfort, equipped for safety and rational operation.

It is not presumed that following this song of praise you will immediately give up your job and become an engine-driver, although the Gornergrat railway would have every reason to be pleased. In spite of this it will do no harm to learn something of the manner of function of a cog railway. Even the passenger should know all about the red button which he, should it be justified and necessary, may press.

Before we use the brakes we must drive. Cog wheel and cog rail are the means by which the motor-coach proceeds on the gradient. The Gornergrat railway is based on the system of the double barred staggered rack developed by Roman Abt which is a further development of the well-known ladder rack of Nikolaus Riggenbach. Abt went from the consideration that two racks are better than one and therefore the safety of the train all the greater the sooner subsequent meshing of the cog wheel with the rack is effected. In order to shorten the intervals he arranged two rack bars in such a way that a gap came to lie next to a tooth. The motor-coach was given corresponding cog wheels with two cog discs which were also staggered by a half a cog partitioning. By placing two double cog wheels one behind the other on two axles and again shifting the mesh by a fraction of second the critical phase of cog-tooth change could be decreased by a quarter over the whole. The ideal size in the design of the cog wheel and the tensile strength of the teeth was a radius of 573 mm. The individual cog wheels are not solidly fixed to the driving axle but are held by springs. By this means an unevenness in the cog rail is taken up and the drive is spared. The carriage obtains an even movement. More than 50 cog-wheel railways over the whole world, from Damascus to Venezuela, are based on the Roman Abt rack-rail system. For his services in the construction of rack railways, Roman Abt was awarded the insignia of a "Knight of the Italian Crown" by the Italian Government in 1895! See page 59 steam locomotive and rail meshing junction for combined traction with cog-wheels and adhesion wheels, pages 60/61 pure cog-wheel

Between Riffelberg station and the last steep slope the Gornergrat railway is double-tracked.
The trains run at short intervals, here two of the twelve two-engined four-axle motor-coaches
Bhe 2/4, built in 1947–1960 cross each other. Present overhead current, 725 Volts.

drive, both in the two-graded rack-rail system of Roman Abt. The Gornergrat
machine was the first electric engine with Abt cog-wheels.

The traction power of the motors is only transmitted to the rack rail by the
cog wheels, cardan-shaft and cardan-joints. The running wheels of motor-
coaches of pure cog railways such as the Gornergrat railway, run free and
are loosely fitted on the driving axles. The double motor-coach has a total of
eight axles arranged in double bogies. Each motor-coach section has its
individual traction apparatus but which is commonly controlled. The coach,
therefore, is only operational as a unit. It may also only be operated as an
individual train and the lower half must always be in the direction of Zermatt.
Each of the bogies has its own driving motor with fitted braking activator
and drive cog wheel. This is always situated on the lower axle às by this
means the teeth are pressed further into the rack rail.

Cog wheel and rack rail are placed higher than running wheel and rail. This results in that, on the one hand the cog wheel is not damaged by the rail bed and on the other hand that the rack rail is led over the rails at points. The upper edge of the rack rail lies 50 mm above that of the rails. Since the radius of the cog wheel and the depth of the insertion of the teeth also have an optimal size it follows that also the running wheels carrying the train must have a set radius. In fact the measurements of cog wheel, cog rail, running wheel and rail interlock like the interlaced form of a puzzle. If a part is deformed by wear so that one can see through the puzzle, the wheels must be replaced, new cog wheels fitted, the cog rails exchanged or the rail re-laid. The tolerances for the individual parts are strictly prescribed.

* 1930 Adaption of the existing four locomotives from 40 Hz to 50 Hz operation, increase of travelling speed to 8.5 km p.h., i.e reduction of travelling time from 80 to 66 minutes. 1939 adaption of number 3 for the transport of material, in 1966 also of No. 1 and 2. 1963 scrapping of No. 5 and 1966 of No. 4.
** 56 seats, remainder standing room;   *** 120 seats, remainder standing room.
Abbreviations see page 48.

Below: The lower (valley-side) bogie of a motor-coach. Right is the three-phase asynchronous motor and the brake drum of the transmission brake on the motor shaft. Left the cardan shaft and the bevel gear transmission. In the middle of the axle the driving cog wheel and in front, the ratchet brake, at the back, transmission housing with the reduction wheels.

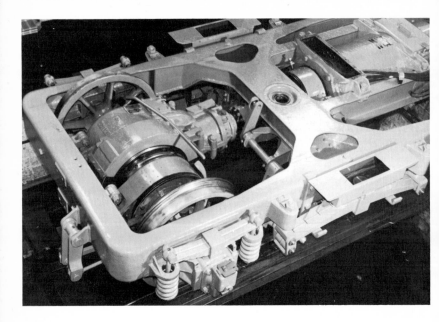

The Traction Vehicles of the Gornergrat Railway (original state)

Rowan trains *	El. engine	El. engine	El. engine
Operating number	1-3	4	5
Operating number since 1964	3001-3003	3004	
Year of construction	1898	1902	1930
Type and series	He 2/2	He 2/2	He 2/2
Driving motors	2	2	2
Traction pinions	2	2	2
Performance per hour, hp	180	180	250
Overall length in m	4,13	4,13	4,13
Weight in tons	10,5	11,5	12,7
Constructor, mech. part	SLM	SLM	SLM
Constructor, elect. part	BBC	BBC	BBC
Ascent and descent, km p.h.	7,2	7,2	8,5
Loaded weight of train, tons	28	29	33
Capacity of train, seats	110	103-110	110
Type-illustration, page	66, 67, 119	68	

1-5

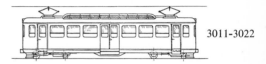

3011-3022

Motor-coaches	Single	Double	
Operating number	101-112		
Operating number since 1964	3011-3022	3041-3042	3043-3044
Year of construction	1947-1960	1965	1974
Type and series	Bhe 2/4	Bhe 4/8	
Driving motors	2	4	
Traction pinions	2	4	
Performance per hour. hp	260	520	
Overall length in m	15,1	30,5	
Weight in tons	17,5	35,3	
Constructor, mech. part	SLM	SLM	
Constructor, elect. part	BBC	BBC	
Ascent and descent, km p.h.	14,5	14,5	
Loaded weight of train, tons	25,6	53,3	
Capacity of train, persons	110 **	230 ***	
Type-illustration, page	85	10, 83, 89	

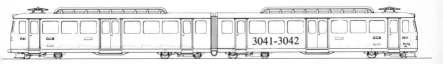

3041-3042

The inside of the brake drum is lined with massive ratchets which can hitch into the locking-pawls. The pawl support is bolted on to the cog wheel hub. The cog wheel can thus turn with the ratchet lining in the uphill direction, that is, the pawls run over the ratchets of the brake. Should, however, for some reason, the vehicle start to run backwards, one of the pawls then locks into the next ratchet. It blocks the cog wheel and stops the train. This is the recoil brake for the ascent. On the double motor-coaches it is automatically set as soon as the engine-driver sets the driving direction switch for the ascent. A green indicator lamp shows that the brakes are in order during the run.

On the descent the ratchet brake is disengaged. In this case it works as the driving brake as a normal brake for holding the train. For normal activation of the mechanical brakes the double motor-coach has an electro-hydraulic apparatus. Pressure is regulated by a small lever. The single motor-coach has spindles, which in order to stop the coach with the ratchet brake requires five revolutions and three for the drive brake. It is clear why the drive brake was fitted as emergency brake at excess speed. It requires less strength. In each section of the double motor-coach the axle of the hill-side bogie drives a centrifugal switch which controls speed. As soon as the maximum permitted speed of 15.2 km per hour is exceeded by 10% it activates braking. The power is stored in child-size loaded springs. Each bogie has its own spring. It is connected to the brake-band of the drive brake by an arrangement of bars and is held in a loaded position by a lock. If one of the centrifugal switches registers excess speed it acts by a magnet on the locking lever of the spring, releases it, the spring unloads and thus tightens the brake-band. At the same time driving current is switched off. The same procedure is given with manual operation of the emergency stop device. The dead-man's pedal, that is the safety device on one-man operation, is connected over a relay with the ratchet brake so that the drive emergency brake is still available as second protection.

The engine-driver is under promise never to use the mechanical brakes on descent as permanent brakes. For this he has the electric brakes. As far as possible he is to drive on the recuperation brake and only for short periods or on a power failure with the resistance brake. The Gornergrat railway has the rare inherent virtue always to run at the prescribed speed (see page 69). This is achieved by the three-phase alternate current induction motors which always try to balance the difference in revolution between the anchor and the rotating field. So long as the frequency of the current network remains constant, the motors keep precisely in time. They literally ride on the back of the frequency; which on its part is regulated by the power station. The constancy of the frequency is regulated here by the most sensitive adjusters.

A double motor-coach Bhe 4/8, built in 1965, at Riffelberg station. The vehicle is in practise a duplication of the single motor-coach except that each section only has one driver's cabin and one pantograph. Loading capacity 18 tons.

On the descent the motors operate with analogue switching as on the ascent as induction generators. On exceeding the idle running speed of 1500 r.p.m. that is at around 14.7 km per hour, they supply braking energy as three-phase current into the overhead line. Now the manager is pleased and the director can laugh: – two trains descending from the mountain practically supply enough power for an uphill train!

The motors are provided with a switching device of a resistor in the armature circuit and thus able to start under greater load than normal. The starting resistors on the roof serve simultaneously as brake resistors. The rotors, that is the rotating parts of the motors, are continuously connected to the starting and braking resistors. They are asymmetrically circuited by the cam-shaft switch-plant in 13 stages. The switchgear is electro-servo-motor operated in the double motor-coach. Each section of the train has its own plant, can, however, only be controlled in common with the other. The operation of the switch elements is effected in proper sequence over the camshaft. On running with network-independent resistance brake the wiring of the fixed motor part, the stator windings, are serially switched with an electro-magnetic switchgear and connected to the parallel working brake activators. The motors now work as outside activated synchronous generators. The D.C. generators, fed from an accumulator battery serve as brake activators which are placed at one end of the driving motor shaft. The complete mechanical braking energy is thus transformed into heat and dissipated by the driving wind from the roof resistors.

Right: The engine's driver view of the descent before the Findelenbach stop.

Bottom right: The hillside driver's cabin of the double motor-coach. The driving control consists of a driving lever with positions 0 to ++, a drive-direction with positions R, O, V and a locking lever. On the left, drive and ratchet brake.

Below: A part of the electric equipment of the double motor-coaches is fitted in the hillside front face of the vehicle. The remaining parts of the electro-hydraulic control equipment are in the middle of the coach and in the lower end face of the carriage.

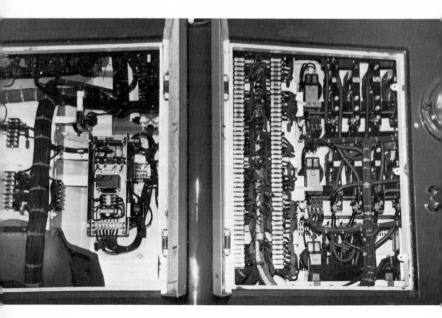

Pistes and Paths

Days on the Gornergrat should figure in your agenda with a thick red line and be noted as special holidays. They stand out from the grey everyday of your calendar as stars in the night and remain unforgettable. This is because the Gornergrat has an incomparable panorama and in addition is an immense playground suited to all requirements. Also the railway has no objection if the freight which it transports makes the very best of the started day to its own desire. For the ones this means photography, filming, sketching and painting with a continually changing foreground and motifs, for the others, silent experience of the moods of the mountains at the edge of the glacier, in the intoxicating beauty of spring flowers or in the last wonderful colours of autumn. The third seek rare plants, animals and rocks and the fourth seek physical relaxation on a hike or by skiing. All is available. It need not always be "Gornergrat return"!

It is certainly not being pedantic if Alpine clubs and hiking societies tell the travellers in any case to take a warm coat, a bite to eat and a map packed in their rucksack for the trip as well as to be fitted out with strong slip-proof boots. The Gornergrat railway ends with its comfortable carriages like a mountain tour, in fresh mountain wind and on steep ground. The hotel is near; but every traveller may have the desire, once arrived, to stretch his legs. Gay and laughing, all care thrown to the winds to expose himself to wind and sun or to go after a picture or a flower. The heedless will soon come to their senses when they retire to bed that evening with a cold or sunburn because they were careless enough to make their reverence to a 3135 metre high mountain in shorts and sandals. Whoever wishes to be carried from the Gornergrat to the Stockhorn will not be able to do without good boots because the track from the top station of the cableway to the summit is a short, safe snow-covered path of 20 minutes. The ride to the Stockhorn opens the view to the Grünsee, Stellisee and Fluhalp and rounds up the panorama to the East of the Gornergrat with a view of the close, immense 20 square kilometres large sea of ice between the Gorner and Findelen glaciers. (Pictures pages 98, 108 and 109). The Stockhorn cable-way claims to be the highest-located in Switzerland.

Inexperienced mountaineers should forget the idea of wanting to go from the Gornergrat to the Stockhorn or vice-versa on foot even if they have got good boots. The little track has numerous easy rock-climbs and requires about two hours walking. Also the crossing of the ridge to the Hohtälli station has a few short parts which require sureness of foot and are not everybody's cup of tea. Thus the possibilities for a continuation of the trip from

Rotenboden station, Riffelhorn. A system of ski-hoists on the West and North slopes of the ridge serve as an extension of the Gornergrat railway and Stockhorn cable-way in a manner that fulfills the skiers' every wish. From November right into summer, easy, medium and difficult runs in many combinations can be made.

the Gornergrat eastwards falls undoubtedly in favour of the silver gondolas which glide along the ridge.

With that, the reserve of the railways is clearly marked and we can now turn to the little black lines on the map showing the hiking paths which do not require any particular alpine expertise. Above all, we study the ways down from the Gornergrat. It is, of course, quite free to the reader to take these paths under his feet in the opposite direction; uphill. Climbing as such is healthier but it requires considerably more energy and at least half as much again in time. In spite of this the hiker will be keen of making the best of the reductions offered by the railway. In this respect he can choose from an innumerable selection of variations so that from any station along the Gornergrat railway he need not take the same path as for the ascent.

Among the Alpine rhododendrons. The modest sheep can still be met on all the alps. The forester does not like to see it in the woods because its grazing hinders the natural rejuvenating of the valuable trees. Also tourists are requested to take care of woods and pastures.

Whoever wishes to return from the Gornergrat Kulm on foot to Zermatt must reckon with a walk of three-and-a-quarter hours. The pistes used by the skiers are not necessarily the best ways. Much prettier are the untouched round-about ways which also are less hard work on the legs; for who wishes to come down to breakfast the next morning with thoroughly painful muscles? Three different paths leave the Gornergrat. The usual and common one, that used in the past by sedan-chair carriers and saddle-horses, runs nearly parallel to the railway line down to the Rotenboden and directly towards the station and hotel Riffelberg (¾ hrs.). From here the path follows on the left of the hotel the flower-edged stream (picture page 116). Quite a way below the railway line it crosses the Riffelbord. After the marshy bowl of Bodmen it drops directly to the site of the earlier Riffelalp hotels (1½ hrs. from the Gornergrat). One should be ware of following, on the right after the

On the Fluhalp beside the moraine of the Findelen glacier the snow is receeding. Adlerhorn and Cima di Jazzi, in between one of the Weisstore. In the shade on the right one of the extensions of the Stockhorn. A ski-tour for the enthousiast: Stockhorn-Cima di Jazzi-Findelen!

Riffelberg, the brightly marked ski-run and the avalanche protection gallery of the railway! Such an undertaking would end in uncomfortable manoeuvres on the path hewn into the steep slope which is only passable in winter and then only for skiers.

In contrast to the described descent which is barely different from the view from the railway, the path along the lakes of the Upper and Lower Kelle (picture page 96) provides a pretty change in scenery. The track leaves the Gornergrat in a northerly direction at the wooden signpost in the bowl beneath the top railway embankment. Arrived at the last little lake and before descending into the Hohtälli the choice is still free to return on this side of the Alp and the Rosenritz over the Gugle to the Riffelberg station. Very pretty, however, is the round-about way over the Grünsee and the Findelen valley (Gornergrat to Grünsee 1½ hrs.). From the Grünsee an even

path, beloved by photographers, through the sparse woods to the Riffelalp station (1 hr.). On both sides of the Findelen stream, paths rich with the scent of resin and honey make their way direct to Winkelmatten and down to Zermatt (1¾ hrs.).

A third path leaves the Gornergrat through the imposing South flank, rich in rare plants and fluttering butterflies. One follows the ridge from the terrace for a distance of 400 m eastwards. Here, a clear small path branches off down to the Gorner glacier. In short, steep but unexposed zig-zags it winds its way quickly down. Just above the moraine it joins the path which leads to the Monte Rosa hut. On this really 'royal' hut-path we return on a level to Rotenboden station (1 hr.). On the way we enjoy the view of the nearly 15 km-long glacier, of the Matterhorn and the Monte Rosa. The way above the edge of the glacier follows a safe little path past the Riffel lakes and the Riffelhorn as far as the Gakihaupt and extends to the Riffelberg station (¾ hrs.). Those who are not worried by the steep slope after the Gakihaupt, may, at the fork of the path, choose the lower and make their way on easy ground to the Riffelalp and the station (¾ hrs.).

The lower path which after the Gakihaupt goes around the Riffelberg and leads to Riffelalp joins, 15 minutes later, the little path descending over the green slope from the Riffelberg hotel in the West. This means that also from the Riffelberg it is not necessary for the return to the valley to follow the pack-horse path and the 'main' road. The little path takes its time and after the crossing with the Gakihaupt path leads even deeper down into the Dristelen. Suddenly it changes its mind, takes a turn to the North and now puts the hiker to the choice, either to make his way on a wide comfortable path on the level to the Riffelalp (from Rotenboden 1½ hrs., from Riffelberg 1 hr.) or to choose the path which leads down to the moraine and to the mouth of the glacier of the Gornera. The path over Boden glacier and Furggbach was once a much used connection between the Riffelalp hotels and Schwarzsee, (picture page 123). For the return to Zermatt one preferably takes the little road as far as Furi. From here the day's march can be ended with a stroll full of diversities along the Gorneren gorge (round-about way Riffelalp-Zermatt 4 hrs.).

The other pretty round-about way from the Riffelalp over the Grünsee and through the Findelen valley we already know (page 95). The direct descent from the Riffelalp to Zermatt over the old pack-horse path touches the

The eye of the deep blue lake in the Upper Kelle below Gornergrat Kulm catches a view of the Feekopf, Allalinhorn, 4027 m, and Rimpfischhorn, 4199 m. In the foreground of the peaks the Schwarzgrat above the Fluhalp. The small path over the Kellen (ladles) and the Hotel Findelen glacier is a favourite variation for the descent to Zermatt (on foot 3¼ hrs.).

Looking into the light of the rising sun, the Stockhorn with the top station of the cable-way at 3405 m and the Cima di Jazzi above the Gorner glacier. View from Gornergrat Kulm. To walk the way from Gornergrat Kulm to the Stockhorn is not recommended to inexperienced mountaineers. It has numerous easy rock-climbs.

Augstchumme and draws a wide loop through the Vorderen Wälder with criss-crossing little tracks (picture page 44). The Alp-path leaves the Riffelalp below the old hotel chapel (1¾ hrs.). A hurried little path branches off from the Riffelalp a few steps below the railway station. It leads through the woods of the Lauberen, steep down to the Findelen stream bridge, passes the power station of the Gornergrat railway and at the bridge before Winkelmatten meets the normal path coming from Riffelalp and Moos (1¼ hrs.).

What would you say to a small trip on the glacier after woods and flowers? Very popular is a visit tc the Monte Rosa hut from the Rotenboden (picture page 100, 2¼ hrs., SAC-hut). A little more demanding – because one must return on the same day – is the tour to the Cima di Jazzi (ascent from the Stockhorn 2 hrs.). Those who like the glaciers traverse the impressive ice-jungle between Rotenboden and Gandegg (2¾ hrs., inn). All glacier tours must be undertaken with good equipment and under knowledgeable guidance. The guides' office in Zermatt regularly organises excursions.

Up to now only walking tours have been discussed. Particular care on the Gornergrat, however, is also given to the maintenance of good ski pistes. Following the second construction stage of the railway, which appeared to be completed with the regular winter operation, a third construction period followed. In 1952 the Gornergrat railway submitted an application to the Federal Department of Railways for the building of a cable-way from the Kulm hotel over the Hohtälli ridge to the Stockhorn. The cable-way with cabins holding 40 people and a running time of 16 minutes was inaugurated on 23. October 1958. It opened up the great skiing area on the North side of the ridge and numerous other ski and mountaineering tours. Because skiers are gripped with the passion of the gliding and swinging art, the Gornergrat railway had to provide a ski-circuit with unlimited possibilities of runs and for the quick transport to the top. This was principally to save the skier an early return to the valley. Besides the track between Riffelberg and Gornergrat Kulm a second track was laid to speed up the traffic. When this was no longer sufficient, various ski-hoists were built on the West and

Popular high alpine tours in the surroundings of the Monte Rosa hut opposite the Gornergrat. The frontier between Switzerland and Italy follows the line between Testa Grigia and Cima di Jazzi. The map shows all huts in the neighbourhood.

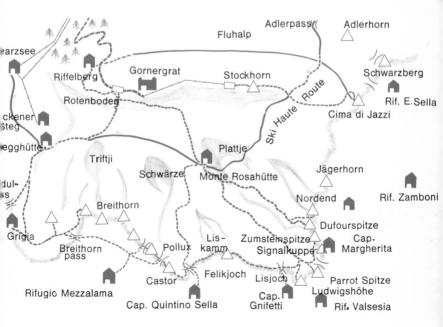

On the ascent to the Monte Rosa hut. Dent d'Hérens, Matterhorn and Dent Blanche are the high peaks on the horizon above the extensive Gorner glacier. From Rotenboden station of the Gornergrat railway the walk takes 2¼ hours.

North slopes to ease up traffic on the railway. They fan out the public brought up by the Gornergrat railway and the Stockhorn cable-way according to their capabilities and snow conditions over the whole back of this mountain. The pistes include easy, medium and difficult runs up to 7 km in length and difference in height of up to 1500 m. The pistes are carefully prepared and maintained by the railways and regularly controlled. It is recommended, prior to the descent, to note the last controlled runs – the times are shown everywhere – and not to leave the marked pistes.

The Fourthousand-metre Peaks seen from the Gornergrat

Summit	Height a.s.l. m	First climbed	Route
Breithorn	4164	1813	from Breithorn pass over SSW-flank
Strahlhorn	4190	1854	from Adler pass over WNW-ridge
Monte Rosa			
Dufourspitze	4634	1855	1. August, over saddle and West ridge (Smyth, Hudson, Birkbeck, Stephenson with guides U. Lauener, J. and M. Zumtaugwald)
Nordend	4609	1861	over Silbersattel and SSW-ridge
Signalkuppe	4556	1842	from Lisjoch over Colle Gnifetti
Allalinhorn	4027	1856	from Allalin pass over South-west ridge
Dom	4545	1858	Festijoch and North-west ridge
Nadelhorn	4327	1858	from Hohbalm glacier over Windjoch
Rimpfischhorn	4199	1859	from Fluh over Rimpfischwang and WSW-ridge
Alphubel	4206	1860	from Alphubeljoch over South-east ridge
Liskamm	4527	1861	from Lisjoch over East ridge
Weisshorn	4505	1861	from Fluh glacier over East ridge
Castor	4228	1861	from Felikjoch over South-east ridge
Täschhorn	4490	1862	over Kin glacier, North-west flank
Dent Blanche	4357	1862	over South ridge
Dent d'Hérens	4171	1863	from South-west over West ridge
Pollux	4092	1864	probably over Schwarztor
Zinalrothorn	4221	1864	from Mountet over North ridge
Obergabelhorn	4063	1865	from Trift over Obergabeljoch
Matterhorn	4477	1865	14. July, from Schwarzsee over Hörnli ridge (Whymper, Hudson, Hadow, Douglas with guides M. A. Croz, Peter Taugwalder father and son)
		1865	17. July, from Breuil over South ridge (guides J. A. Carrel und J. B. Bich)
		1879	Zmutt ridge
		1899	Furggen ridge
		1931	North wall
		1965	Diretissima
Hohberghorn	4219	1869	from Stecknadeljoch over ESE-ridge
Lenzspitze	4294	1870	from Nadeljoch over North-west ridge
Dürrenhorn	4035	1879	from Dürrenjoch over North ridge
Bishorn	4153	1884	from Bisjoch

Following pages: View from Gornergrat Kulm to the North-West. On the extreme left above the lichen-covered rocks, Dent Blanche, then Grand Cornier and the beautiful group of the Obergabelhorn-Wellenkuppe. Below the Gabelhorn glacier, the ragged peaks of the Unter-gabelhorn. Extending beyond the edge of the picture, the ridge from the Trifthorn to the Zinal Rothorn, popular with good climbers. Right, the striking triangle of the Weisshorn and immediately below it the tame but worth-while Mettelhorn. →

Rock-Climbing-Garden beside the Railway

A small mountain, very full of itself; that is the Riffelhorn. It is not for nothing that this little chap, drawing up his shoulder, cheekily, as if it had studied itself in the mirror of the Riffel lake, takes a pose of the Matterhorn and places itself in front of this mighty mountain.

The easiest way to reach the 2927 m high Riffelhorn is from the Rotenboden station in about one hour. The climb, however, includes half-an-hour of solid rock-climbing. The mountain is not climbed without rope and colleagues. The beginner may honestly admit to be scared when he is first put on the rope. Those liable to giddiness may also admit to be impressed by the view down on to the Gorner glacier. There is probably no guide who would not enjoy the little joke to leave his charge clinging in the chimney of the Skyline for a while and let him wobble on the narrow edge which separates the safe hold in the Serpentine from the airy nothing. For it is in this way that the distribution of the roles in the rope are made very clear and the pupil learns what the rescuing hand of the guide is worth. The Riffelhorn is the test whether one is up to the hardships of an ascent of the Matterhorn and that one can stand the heights which need to be overcome.

The easier routes on to the Riffelhorn are all on the North side about 170 metres above the Riffel lake. Its high face of 400 m, however, is turned to the glacier. Its West wall is gutted by vertical cracks and a large couloir.

Whoever wishes to ascend the Matterhorn will usually first be thoroughly tested on the Riffelhorn by his guide. As unpretentious as it looks, the Riffelhorn has a whole series of climbing routes. The interesting ones are on the side facing the Matterhorn. The side with the easier routes face the Riffel lake and Rotenboden station. They are classified according to difficulty as follows: Normal route (A), Seeweg (B), Skyline (C). The belaying route (D) is only used for the descent.

Well-known is the "Matterhorn-couloir" which is considered as very difficult and flat directly opposite the Matterhorn. In the South wall are the closely together, rarely climbed routes demanding highest requirements to the expertise of climbers; the Grogan couloir, the Eck, the Glacier couloir, the Edge, the Biner couloir and the Thermometer couloir. The day's program of a good climber may include three to four various routes. For those who believe in training and also do not wish to be idle in poor weather conditions there is thus a practise instrument right next to the tracks of the Gornergrat railway.

Gornergrat Clear

It is only proper to spare a few words on the choice of the right day for a trip to the Gornergrat. Any day is alright if it promises to be a fine one. This is not difficult to have in Zermatt but it is better not to leave the last day of the holidays for the Gornergrat but to make use right away of the first period of fine weather. The view is most impressive early in the morning when the inclining shadows of the clear sun bring the clefts of the mountains into well-defined relief. The successive ridges are now sharply staggered and the summits are distinctly to be seen by the naked eye in their topographically correct position. In the heat of midday the dust-saturated layers of the atmosphere climb up the valley and lie as a thin curtain in front of the picture. They turn the mountain ranges into a surface in which the glaciers stand out with a practically intolerable brilliance and formlessness. Later in the afternoon as soon as the air cools off and settles, the sun has ended its arch, the mountains and snows again increase in relief and splendour. It is therefore recommended to take one of the first trains in the morning to the Gornergrat or at least to arrange matters in such a way that one need only return to the valley by the last train in the evening.

Let us remain with the weather: A boring subject of conversation in Zermatt – it is practically always fine. But in spite of this it is a highly interesting topic. Why is it always fine? In order to understand this we must return to our special case of the Monte Rosa (page 12). This mountain wall does not only provide its neighbours' pastures with avalanches and scree, it also collects the raindrops out of the damp mass of air and leads them into the basin of Macugnaga and Alagna. The vapours carried from the Adriatic and from the Mediterranean rise up the East face of the Monte Rosa, cool off and – when for once they have to – let the water simply drop on the border ridge. Zermatt remains dry. In the South and South-West the Zermatter bowl borders on the high Piedmontese Alps and the Aosta valley which also has a dry climate. The damp atmosphere coming from the Mediterranean into the country is considerably cooled off before it reaches the Zermatt border on the southerly and westerly mountain ridges and deposits precipitations there.

The rock fingers of the Mischabel and the snow-covered dome of the Alphubel, 4206 m, rise over the Unter and Ober Rothorn on the side of the Fluhalp. In the middle of the picture in the sun, the long Teufelsgrat (Devil's ridge) on the Täschhorn, 4490 m. Next to it in the shade, the Dom, 4545 m, and just visible the Nadelgrat with (from left to right) Dürrenhorn, 4035 m, Hohberghorn, 4219 m, and Stecknadelhorn, 4242 m. View from Gornergrat Kulm.

With the Gornergrat-Stockhorn cable-way a further rise of 250 metres is achieved over the Hohtälli ridge into the world of the glaciers. Directly below the Matterhorn, Gornergrat Kulm.

Clouds in the mountains are usually the result of rising damp atmosphere from the valley. As we have seen, during the course of the day, atmospheric layers saturated with water vapour rise from the bottom of the valley (picture page 98). This movement is accompanied by a cooling off and condensation of dampness which leads to cauliflower-like massed clouds. These towering cumuli are characteristic for the border ridges of the Pennine Alps (picture pages 40/41). If the weather is dry and fine they are over the border ridge, if it is damp, they embrace the summits and often rid themselves of their load in a thundrous shower in that place. Rarely – only in pronounced pressure conditions – do the cloud-banks lying in the gaps of the passes advance to the inner region of Zermatt.

It follows therefore that Zermatt is completely closed off in an extraordinary manner against the rain-bringing South, South-East and South-West winds by its high ramparts and yet its glaciers are fed. In nine out of ten cases when

View from Stockhorn station of Castor, Pollux and Breithorn. At the bottom left the ragged Gorner glacier and the "Plattje" where the Monte Rosa hut is situated.

clouds can be seen on the horizon they keep to the great mountain chains around the valley and leave the centre alone. On the sides, the gigantic ridges of the Mischabel, the Weisshorn and the Dent Blanche hold up the damp blessing (see map page 7). In these circumstances plants and animals find particularly favourable living conditions and are to be found at greater heights than in the rest of the Alps. The tree-line is at 2300 m, the snow-line at 3000 to 3250 m, blossom plants can be found up to over 3500 m. The mountain spring is, depending on the height, between May and July.

It is not surprising that the Gornergrat, sitting in the centre of the dry atmospheric area is satisfactory for the astronomers who avoid the dust and vapour-saturated atmospheric layers of the plains with their instruments. The Kulm hotel, belonging to the Zermatt burghers, accommodates two observatories from which international groups of scientists study the sky by day and by night (pictures pages 10 and 110). The domes are to be enlarged at

The astronomers' dome on the North tower of Gornergrat Kulm built in 1967 by the Astronomical Institute of Oxford University in order to undertake surveys of the sun. The dome on the South tower built in 1966 is used by French astronomers and scientists of the Geneva Observatory.

present and to be supplied with stronger instruments for the Universities of Milan, Rome and Lyon. One of the telescopes is to have a diameter of 150 cm and thus will be the largest instrument at such a height in Europe.

The relation of summer precipitations to those of winter is very balanced in Zermatt. The driest is February and October is the wettest. Naturally the central area of the Pennine Alps, the group around the Monte Rosa, is subject to the natural laws of snowfall. Zermatt, however, has slightly less snow than the Northern chains but the skier can reckon with greater certainty with fine weather. While grey fog covers the plain, blue sky is over Zermatt. Usually it is the North wind which brings the white blessing over the Gemmi and Turtmann valley into the lower part of the Visper valleys while the great load of snow is brought by the damp winds from the Adriatic and the Mediterrannean and reaches the upper Saas valley and through the gates of the passes into the Zermatter bowl. It must also be realised that normally there is less snow on the summits than in the valley. The winter winds and storms blow the white magic from the mountain ridges with the same diligence as city road-sweepers wipe it from the streets. Before one has rubbed one's eyes to enjoy the fresh snow, it has already been cleared away. Only in April or even in May the Alps really become snowbound. Under the growing strength of the sun the snow clings better, it turns into eternal snow which can not be shifted by the winds. The rounding grains of the eternal snow is the first step of ice-formation. On the glaciers they melt over midday to a regular soft layer. May and June are therefore the golden times for the Spring skier. At this period also the crevasses on the glaciers are covered with strong snow-bridges and are the least dangerous.

Someone who has great experience of the snow conditions in the high Alps is the mountain Ibex. While the Chamois prefer the upper parts of the woods in winter and sometimes directly risk the danger of avalanches, the Ibex seeks the safe rock above the highest trees. As soon as the snow falls, this animal feels itself safe on the hard rock above the frozen streams and rivulets. It has a preference for the South slopes which are cleared of snow by the sun and wind sooner than other slopes. With their hooves, the animals scratch out the grass and herbs. Otherwise they scratch lichen from the rocks and live on their fat which they have accumulated during the summer. As soon as the thaw sets in and the alps start to become green, the Ibex return to the lower reaches and to the freshly laid table. At this period, mid-May to mid-June, their young are born.

The Ibex likes company and lives in herds (picture page 33, photographed early in July), so that priority of rank can be established in peace and small fights before the rutting time sets in in December and January. At about the end of July the males separate from the rabble – the females and kids – and vanish in groups of ten or twenty. The summer brings a wider distribution of the animals. The males who have rid themselves of their heavy winter coats feel lively and free and remain at a height of 2600 to 3000 m. The females and younger animals stay lower down. Humans are regarded with innocent amber eyes. At the slightest nervous movement of such a two-legged being, however, the animal prefers to show its backside and, with lifted tail to show those following the direction of his retreat, makes for the hills. The climbing art of these heavy animals is surprising. Their short tough, sinewy legs enable them to jump up 4 to 5 metre-high walls without a start and with complete disconcern, spreading their front hooves to hold on to ridges not wider than a finger. Nevertheless one is well advised to leave the Ibex in peace and never to remain below them. They can very easily loosen rocks.

It is most likely their fearlessness led to the Ibex becoming a too easy victim of the hunter. At the beginning of the last Century the animal was completely extirpated in Switzerland and in the Tirol and only after wearisome and numerous unsuccessful attempts it was slowly possible to repatriate the mountain Ibex with last pairs from the Gran Paradiso back to his native

Vehicles and Performance of the Brig-Visp-Zermatt Railway

Years	Steam engines	Electric engines	Double motor- coaches	Train-km av. p. year	Passengers conveyed, av. p. year	Goods tons, av. p. year
1890-1907	4-7	—	—	42 918	54 166	5 905
1908-28	8	—	—	48 728	68 538	7 154
1929-38	3-1	5	—	115 642	146 357	11 324
1939-59	1	6	—	209 966	368 572	29 995
1960-65	1	6	2	473 870	993 836	84 379
1966-72	1	6	5	605 677	1 427 278	70 969

Capacity 1900, 570 seats; 1972, 2 912 seats.

land and in carefully chosen reservations. Today the Ibex is under full protection in Switzerland.

The ignorance of humanity is unlimited. One would imagine that the obvious, poor experience with this beautiful wild animal should have been a warning to reason as early as 200 years ago. But no, even with butterfly net and botanist's case – today it would be plastic bags – camouflaged as naturalists man cannot resist to rob the valleys and the mountains of their rare treasures. The Gornergrat holds gems, among others glacial relics whose names one dare not mention in order not to risk subjecting them to frivolous search and subsequent extinction. If the burghers of Zermatt, to whom the mountain belongs, were not already aware what the beauty of the mountain is worth and took corresponding care of it, the Gornergrat would have to be sold to the World Wildlife Fund and placed under its protection.

Believe it or not: – shortly before the first World War there existed entomologists who turned over every rock on the Rotenboden and systematically destroyed caterpillars and chrysalis attached to the small plants underneath them of a 3 cm-moth in order to increase the Gold-Mark price of the preserved specimens in the collections ten-fold! Around 1900 the chestnut-brown butterfly was often to be seen between Riffelberg and Rotenboden; however, since it was discovered that this specimen was unique in the World and has no contemporary in Siberia or in Central Asia, a proper hoarding-hunt set in for the animal by insect dealers. A close relation of the small butterfly can be found on the Gornergrat and at similar Alpine levels as well as in Lapland

and in Siberia. As these finds barely showed different characteristics, the zoologists established that 60 000 years did not suffice to develop an own species.

Similar observations were announced by the botanists and it was they who first drew attention to the Gornergrat. They found plants which only grew here, others which are also native to the high North. This led to the presumption that during the last Ice-period, when the Polar glacier reached down to Berlin – and the Alpine ice crust reached as far as Frankfurt, the Gornergrat had had a favoured climate. Some humps and rock protrusions may have already jutted from the ice and were spoilt by the sun in such a way that plants and animals could survive in the cracks and little ravines which otherwise can nowhere be found. Our small cold-sustaining moths may have survived on such humps or they may have found their way back to the Alps from the Tundra between the two great ice covers during the course of thousands of years while their more widely distributed relations followed the retracting ice to the North as well as to the South.

Butterfly life does not by any means stop at the line of the eternal snows. It manages to sustain in the Zermatt area on little green islets above 3700 metres. Butterflies are known which pass their whole development and their whole life within the snow-line. Above a height of 1500 metres, however, they are often satisfied with only one hatch per year. Some require several years for their development. Plant life is analogue. Interesting collections can be found in the Alpine Museum of Zermatt.

The steam train puffs along
St. Niklaus on its way to Zermatt
with open summer carriages beyond.

Climatically and floristically the Valais centre forms a unit with the adjacent south-westerly long low Alpine valleys of the Piedmont and the Dauphiné. The inner Valais is characterised by the almost complete barrier from the north-westerly Atlantic air currents. In the North the rain-bringing winds are stopped by the majestic chain of the Bernese Alps, in the West the barrier of the Dents-du-Midi and the Dents-de-Morcles. In the South, as we already know, the Pennine Alps hold up the air currents from the Adriatic and the

Tariffs		1898	1974
Zermatt - Gornergrat	return fare	Fr. 18.—	Fr. 29.—
Visp - Zermatt	return fare		
	2nd. class	Fr. 18.—	Fr. 28.—
	1st. class	Fr. 28.80	Fr. 42.—

Mediterranean. The result is a highly reduced precipitation, great clearness of the sky, a continuous sun-radiation and considerable drying-out with constant valley winds. In contrast to northerly Switzerland, the Valais does not have a climate of Oceanic and Mediterranean character but the feature of the Continental climate with a rapid increase of heat in the spring and summer. In addition, the heat radiation and drying on the southerly and northerly exposed valley slopes is almost similar.

Decisive for plant life is not the temperature but the degree of dryness. The beech forest with its typical flora prevailing in the plains and hilly parts of

Pack-horses in front of the stables of the hotel Riffelberg.

The hamlet Findelen where grain ripens at 2200 metres.

Switzerland is completely lacking in the central Valais. Pine is extensive. In the upper Nikolai valley birch and above all larch and cembra-pine are frequent. The woods are accompanied by plants, Xerophytes, who in view of their special capability to grow on sunny and sparse top-soil slopes and rocks are satisfied with short periods of soaking. It is peculiar that the dry plants and rock-heather suddenly start at the barrier before the knee of the Rhone but carry on a lively exchange with the neighbourly plant-life over the high passes of Zermatt into the Aosta valley. The Nikolai valley appears to carry out the "clearing"-business in the Valais plant-life. Although Zermatt lies 1000 metres higher than the climatically favoured Sion it does not have a considerably higher precipitation. At Stalden is the point with the lowest record of rain-fall in Switzerland. The almost similar amount of precipitation in Sion as in Zermatt explains the possibility of existence of the flora adjusted to dryness in the height as well as in the plain and thus the crossing of the Pennine border ridge.

The botanists believe that the Gornergrat has the greatest number of types of flora in the Valais because the various plant societies – Alpine flowers, Xerophytes, glacial relics, Hybrids – overlap in the best possible conditions. Think of the promotion of blossom-forming by the strong ultra-violet light, the preserving heat and water-regulation by the surrounding glaciers, the tree-line at great height, the clear sky. "Hikers, botanists, entemologists who enter the valley floor of Zermatt, a new world opens up to you. A world full of sun and brilliance, full of the light of the snows and defiant rock formations. Wherever you tread, your foot sinks into the flower carpet of the Alpine pastures and butterflies flutter around you in a variety of types which will not easily be found again in the high Alps". May one today still quote these words of a scientist without adding the warning in the same breath: "yes, but only to look at"? We know today that only the picking of a few blossoms of a flower from its native habitat, robs it of its possibility of defense against invasion of another type; and only the finest specimens are picked. Even more depressing for the flower friend is the necessity in recent years of re-laying of the waters, the consequences of which, for the vegetation, may not be foreseen.

Riffelberg above the Nikolai valley around 1900. The Riffelhaus built in 1854 (with wood skirtings under the eaves) had to be extended already a few summers later and is still today externally barely changed, a well-kept hotel.

Grandfather at the Telescope

As little as the Valais fits into the climate and the plant life of northern Switzerland, was it included in its economy. The Valaisans liked to take the path of the flowers and for the supply of the necessities of life – and its luxuries – used the gates to the South. The Valais holds the important mountain passes at the Simplon and the Grand St-Bernard over which the big transit traffic was effected since ancient times between the western and southerly neighbours. Also the Monte Moro and Theodul were used when it was found necessary to fill cellar and shed or to sell goods. The connections over the northern and eastern Alpine chain – Furka, Grimsel, Lötschen, Gemmi and Rawyl – corresponded more to the law of political sense and safety and led an existence in the shade of the small neighbourly mercenary trade. "Foot-travel is of course tiring but only with the certain difference that in a mountainous country it is by far not so tiresome than in the plain" comforted an advisor on the useful and pleasurable way to travel in Switzerland. "The continual change on the path on which one ascends and descends,

The top station of the Gornergrat railway originally lay 70 metres lower down than it does today, in a depression. On sedan chairs and on horses, ladies and invalids were transported up the last slope. Prior to the construction of the railway this was the common means of transport from Zermatt.

then continues straight on, helps that soon this, or that muscle is set into lively activity and exertion while those which were previously taxed can have somewhat of a rest by less activity; in short, not always the same muscles are exerted as is the case on a level road. The extraordinary effect of the invigorating pure mountain air on the human machine considerably facilitates travel in the mountains."

When the flow of travellers started in Zermatt and on the Riffelberg, the only available means of regular transport between the Lake of Geneva and Domodossola to Visp at the entrance to the mountain valley was by postal

Above: Simultaneously with the Monte Rosa hut (previously Bétemps hut) the "Hotel Belvédère" was inaugurated in 1895 on the dome of the Gornergrat. 15 years later the building had already been torn down, the view cleared and the Kulm hotel was erected below the highest point in its present position.

Right: Gornergrat station in the inauguration year in 1898. Shortly afterwards the line was extended by the embankment which leads up to the new hotel. 1909 the new station was opened, which like the hotel, is built in English castle style.

coach. A year after Whymper's ascent of the Matterhorn the stage-coach on the newly paved Furka road provided a connection with Central Switzerland and the Gotthard and it was only twelve years later that the first railway train steamed up the marshy Rhone plain from Sion towards the small town of Visp of the Jura-Simplon railway which was under construction. When the rack-and-pinion railway to Zermatt was already accepted as a matter of course, there was still no connection to the North over the mountains. The road over the Grimsel pass was opened for coach traffic in 1895 and the Lötschberg railway started operation shortly before the outbreak of the First World War and seven years after the piercing of the first Simplon tunnel. Our grandparents, therefore, had a considerably tiresome journey to the newly discovered, wonderful world on the Gornergrat and fully indulged in the hospitality which was provided there.

Until 1838 it was a common habit to knock on the parson's door if one wanted a bed for the night. The Valais Government, however, considered this custom as unsuitable and stopped the clerics from doing so without further ado. It is well known that pastors were not born yesterday and if Zermatt today enjoys a blossoming hotel trade, then it is only thanks to their pastor Joseph Ruden and the young chaplain Joseph Seiler. Seiler wrote to his brother: "Last year there were a considerable number of travellers and all

Next pages: Gornergrat Kulm with the old Hotel Belvédère around 1900. Left, the Lower Theodul glacier, in front of the Matterhorn the plateau of the Upper Theodul glacier. →

agree on the beauty of the area and say that Zermatt has, until now, not been known. It will now become ever more popular and will be visited in summer by ever more people." Many had expressed the desire that if there was only an inn on that mountain called the Riffel, from where there is the most beautiful view!

The brother, Alexander Seiler, did not long hesitate and one day he arrived with his belongings. Ruden organised the carpenters and masons and saw to it that the new Riffelhaus remained the property of the Burghers' Commune and that a lease was established with Alexander Seiler. The enterprise did so well that others soon followed: In the valley, at Schwarzsee, the Riffelalp and in the Goms. What, however, the young topographer, Xaver Imfeld, was looking for when, in the SAC yearbook of 1881, he described his night's stay at Baltschieder, he did not deign to mention: "When, during the night I looked through the telescope I noticed light in the Riffel hotel; probably they were having breakfast in order to pay an early morning call on one of my old acquaintances on the Gorner glacier. The direct distance from here to Riffel is no less than 43 km. If I possessed a stronger telescope, my indiscreet observations would be enriched by far beyond the interesting details on the appetite and the quality of the breakfast of my microscopic society at Riffel." It is the story of the frog who is transformed to a Prince and the brown-eyed maiden. One of Alexander Seiler and his worldly wife Catherine's fourteen children became Imfeld's wife, himself attaining international reknown through his work.

Where can this decrepit line lead to? It used to connect the Riffelalp station of the Gornergrat railway with the 500 metre southerly luxury Hotel Seiler at Riffelalp. The quaint vehicle was operated by three-phase alternate current and was considered as unique among Europe's trams: It operated on the shortest and highest track. A carriage carried ten people.

After the fire of the luxury hotel – it had 120 rooms – the little railway lost its existence. How and when the hotel should be rebuilt is still open.

In the bottom right of the picture is the packhorse track and the loop of the Gornergrat railway between Riffelberg and Riffelalp. Right in the corner, the hotel.

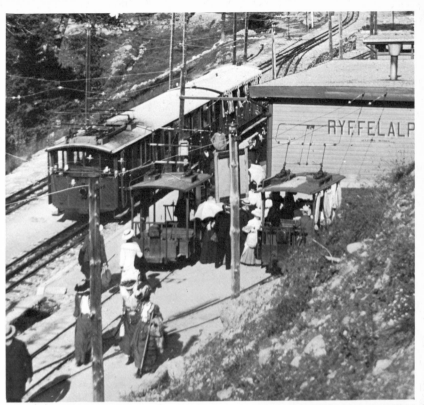

Une rue à Zermatt

L. Yedi! Morgen nehmen wir
Abschied von diesem bekannten
Orte. Grüsse von Peja & Mac

However, when Imfeld had his idea for the Gornergrat railway it was necessary to tread very softly. He was obliged to stand in Heer's shadow in order not to cause unnecessary trouble. "The Gornergrat railway originated from my own initiative. I was also here the originator of the project and together with the late Mr. Heer-Bétrix of Bienne, concessionary", he wrote many years later in his application for an electric narrow-gauge rack-and-pinion railway between Brig and Gletsch. The successful father-in-law, Alexander Seiler, had the embarrassing misfortune not to be a native of Zermatt. He was born on the wrong side of the valley but had the sincere desire to be buried as a Zermatter. We know Zermatt: The wish was tardily fulfilled. Mrs. Maria Imfeld-Seiler, however, remained for many years after the death of her husband as manageress of the two hotels, Zermatterhof and Monte Rosa. Did you perhaps still know her?

Post-card greetings in the year 1905. The "Viehgasse" (cattle-track) with the angled stables and sheds still exists today. Also the vicarage and the Hotel Monte Rosa at bottem left, look unchanged upon the carefree strolling tourists. The generation is new but Zermatt has retained its charm. We shall come again!

asse in Zermatt

Une rue à Zermat

Historical Index

999 The last king of High Burgundy presents the "Country Valais" to the Bishop of Sion. The republic of the "Zenden" is formed.

1538–1618 The Zermatters purchase their freedom of person and belongings from their masters and form three independent republics.

1791 The three Zermatt Communes unite to one.

1798 Napoleon invades the Valais, inclusion in the Helvetian Republic. 1802 severence and establishment of an independent republic. 1810 annexation by France and liberation by Austrian regiments.

1815 The Valais joins the Swiss Confederation.

Around 1830 the first tourists in Zermatt and on the Riffelberg.

1852 Alexander Seiler leases the small inn "Monte Rosa" with three guest beds from the surgeon Lauber.

1854 Inauguration of the "Riffelhaus" at Riffelalp. 1864, extension.

1855 First ascent of the highest summit in Switzerland (1.8.), the Dufourspitze in the Monte Rosa massif, from the Riffelhaus.

1855 Zermatt already records 90 hotel beds.

1865 First ascent of the Matterhorn by Whymper (10.7.)

1878 Alexander Seiler opens the guesthouse Riffelalp. 1884 opening of the newly built Hotels Seiler at Riffelalp (10.7.)

1886 Charles Masson and Konrad Gysin are granted the concession for the construction of a railway from Visp to Zermatt (21.12.) on behalf of a company to be formed with headquarters in Lausanne. Operation from 1. May to 1. October.

1890 Inauguration of the railway as far as St. Niklaus (22.8.), 1891 as far as Zermatt (6.7.)

1890 Concession application Caspar Leonhard Heer for the construction of a railway to the Gornergrat and the Matterhorn (20.8.). The participation of Xaver Imfeld in the application is recorded in contracts of 27.2.; 3.3. and 15.8.1890. Heer dies in December, the legatees take over the rights.

1890 Concession application for the same project (22.9.) by Jean Ant. Roten, S. Zen Ruffinen and von Ernst, banker in Bern.

1892 The Federal Parliament grant building permit for the Gornergrat and Matterhorn railways to Imfeld and Heer (20.6.) on behalf of a joint stock company to be formed with headquarters in Sion.

1894 Imfeld cedes his share of the concession to August Haag, architect (30.1.). Haag forms a firm with Karl Greulich in the same year, and takes over the construction of the Gornergrat railway under contract.

1895 Opening of Bétemps hut, later new construction of Monte Rosa hut.

1895 Opening of Hotel Belvédère on Gornergrat. It is pulled down in 1910.

1895 Federal decree concerning non-intervention on the application for extension of the term for the Matterhorn railway (16.12.).

1896 Approval of the altered plans for Gornergrat railway (1.4.). Work is started mid-May.

1896 Founding of the joint stock company of the Gornergrat railway (11.6.)

1897 First trial run of a composition of the Gornergrat railway, the first electric rack-and-pinion locomotive in Switzerland (24.11.).

1898 Inauguration of the Gornergrat railway (20.8.). For the present the season lasts from beginning June to beginning October.

1906 Opening of the Simplon tunnel.

1909 Extension of the end of the line of the Gornergrat railway. 1910 opening of the new Kulmhotel Gornergrat owned by the Burghers' Commune.

1913 Opening of the Lötschberg tunnel.

1914 Opening of the Furka-Oberalp railway as far as Oberwald. 1926 as far as Disentis.

1920 The Visp-Zermatt railway turns to individual operation. It was previously operated by the Federal railways and before that by the Jura-Simplon railway.

1921 Operating agreement of the Gornergrat railway with the Visp-Zermatt railway on joint operation.

1929/30 For the first time the Gornergrat railway runs in winter as far as Riffelalp.

1929/30 The Visp-Zermatt railway is extended to Brig, renamed and electrified.

1930 Adaption of the Gornergrat railway from 40 to 50-cycle operation.

1933 The Brig-Visp-Zermatt railway starts all-year-round operation.

1946 Completion of the avalanche gallery Riffelbord.

1947 The Gornergrat railway purchases light-weight motor-coaches.

1954 Granting of concession to the Gornergrat railway for the cable-way to the Stockhorn (18.8.).

1956 Inauguration of the first section of the cable-way, 1958 second section.

1961 The main building of the hotels Riffelalp is completely destroyed by fire.

1965 The Gornergrat railway purchases double motor-coaches.

1966 Construction of the astronomical dome on the South tower of the Kulm hotel and installation of a 40-cm telescope. 1967 construction of the second dome.

1974 Extension of the astronomical observation stations at Gornergrat Kulm and installation of a 150-cm telescope.

Index of Tables

Maps and Reliefs

Without the active support of the Gornergrat railway this book would not have been written. The author extends her thanks to the Board of Directors, in particular to its Chairman Mr. H. Römer as well as to Director A. Binz for their trust. The thanks also go to all the assistants who always helped in a most friendly way with information that was required.

Illustrations: Swissair, page 12; Kur- und Verkehrsverein Zermatt, pages 21, 24/25, 40/41, 108, 109; Rudolf Zimmermann 78, 80, 83, 86, 90, 91; Geneva University 110; Edmund Wunderlich 8/9; Swiss Locomotive and Machine Works Winterthur 49, 87. The historical illustrations are taken from the archives of the Gornergrat railway and from old publications. The cover pictures, colour photographs, maps and other photographs are by the author. An indication of sources of information would unfortunately lead too far as such a list would include well over a hundred titles.